It's a brilliant development from CGP!

GCSE Edexcel B Geography is all about people and the environment...
and naturally there are plenty of tricky questions in the new Grade 9-1 exams.

Not to worry. This CGP book is bursting with exam-style practice for every
topic — perfect for making sure you're ready for the real thing.

We've even included some practice for the new fieldwork
and decision-making questions. Everything you need to shore up
your knowledge and coast through the exams.

CGP — still the best! ☺

Our sole aim here at CGP is to produce the highest quality books —
carefully written, immaculately presented and dangerously close to being funny.

Then we work our socks off to get them out to you
— at the cheapest possible prices.

Contents

✓ Use the tick boxes to check off the topics you've completed.

Getting Started

How to Use this Book 1
Exam Breakdown 2
Answering Questions 3

Component 1: Global Geographical Issues

Topic 1 — Hazardous Earth

Global Atmospheric Circulation 4
Natural Climate Change 6
Climate Change — Human Activity 7
Tropical Cyclones 9
Tropical Cyclones — Impacts 10
Tropical Cyclones — Preparation and Responses 11
Structure of the Earth 12
Plate Boundaries 13
Volcanic Hazards 14
Earthquake Hazards 15
Impacts of Tectonic Hazards 16
Management of Tectonic Hazards 17

Topic 2 — Development Dynamics

Measuring Development 18
Global Inequalities 20
Theories of Development 22
Globalisation 23
Reducing Global Inequalities 24
Development in Emerging Countries 25

Topic 3 — Challenges of an Urbanising World

Urbanisation 28
Cities — Growth and Decline 29
Urban Economies 30
Urban Change 31
Urban Land Use 32
Urban Change in Megacities 33

Component 2: UK Geographical Issues

Topic 4 — The UK's Evolving Physical Landscape

Rocks and the UK Physical Landscape 37
Landscape Processes — Physical 39
Landscape Processes — Human 40

Coastal Change and Conflict

Coastal Weathering and Erosion 41
Coastal Landforms 42
Human Activity at the Coast 45
Coastal Flooding 47
Coastal Management 48

River Processes and Pressures

River Processes and Landscapes 49
River Landforms 51
River Landscapes and Sediment Load 54
River Discharge and Flooding 55
River Management 57
Investigating a UK Geographical Issue 58

Topic 5 — The UK's Evolving Human Landscape

UK Human Landscape 59
Migration 61
The UK Economy 62
UK Links with the Wider World 63
Dynamic UK Cities 64

Topic 6 — Geographical Investigations

Fieldwork in a Physical Environment 67
Investigating Coastal Change and Conflict ... 69
Investigating River Processes and Pressures .. 70
Fieldwork in a Human Environment 71
Investigating Dynamic Urban Areas 73
Investigating Changing Rural Areas 74

Component 3:
People and Environment Issues — Making Geographical Decisions

Topic 7 — People and the Biosphere

Global Ecosystems 75
Humans and the Biosphere 78
Role of the Biosphere 79
Demand for Resources 80

Topic 8 — Forests Under Threat

Tropical Rainforests 81
Threats to Tropical Rainforests 83
Tropical Rainforests — Conservation 84
Taiga Forests 86
Threats to Taiga Forests 88
Taiga Forests — Conservation 89

Topic 9 — Consuming Energy Resources

Impacts of Energy Production 90
Access to Energy 92
Oil Supply and Demand 93
Increasing Energy Supply 94
Sustainable Energy Use 95
Energy Futures 96

Making a Geographical Decision

Making a Geographical Decision 98

Published by CGP

Editors:
Ellen Burton, Chris McGarry, Claire Plowman, Hannah Roscoe, David Ryan.

With thanks to Susan Alexander and Karen Wells for the proofreading.

With thanks to Ana Pungartnik for copyright research.

ISBN: 978 1 78294 622 9

Clipart from Corel®
Printed by Elanders Ltd, Newcastle upon Tyne

Based on the classic CGP style created by Richard Parsons.

Text, design, layout and original illustrations © Coordination Group Publications Ltd. (CGP) 2017
All rights reserved.

Photocopying this book is not permitted. Extra copies are available from CGP with next day delivery.
0800 1712 712 • www.cgpbooks.co.uk

Getting Started

How to Use this Book

- Hold the book <u>upright</u>, approximately <u>50 cm</u> from your face, ensuring that the text looks like <u>this</u>, not s!ɥʇ. Alternatively, place the book on a <u>horizontal</u> surface (e.g. a table or desk) and sit adjacent to the book, at a distance which doesn't make the text too small to read.
- In case of emergency, press the two halves of the book together <u>firmly</u> in order to close.
- Before attempting to use this book, familiarise yourself with the following <u>safety information</u>:

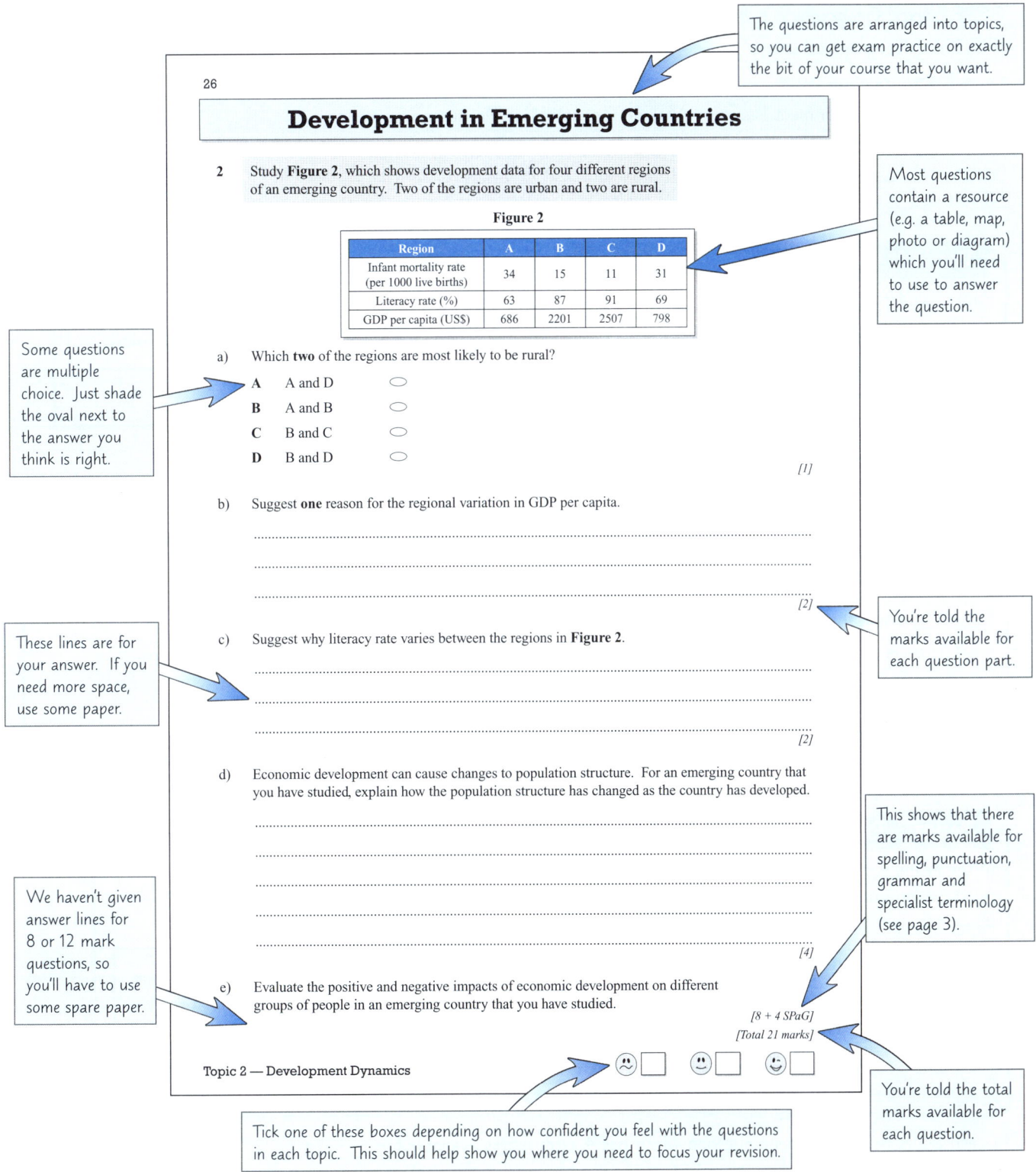

The questions are arranged into topics, so you can get exam practice on exactly the bit of your course that you want.

Most questions contain a resource (e.g. a table, map, photo or diagram) which you'll need to use to answer the question.

Some questions are multiple choice. Just shade the oval next to the answer you think is right.

These lines are for your answer. If you need more space, use some paper.

You're told the marks available for each question part.

This shows that there are marks available for spelling, punctuation, grammar and specialist terminology (see page 3).

We haven't given answer lines for 8 or 12 mark questions, so you'll have to use some spare paper.

You're told the total marks available for each question.

Tick one of these boxes depending on how confident you feel with the questions in each topic. This should help show you where you need to focus your revision.

Exam Breakdown

Welcome to the wonderful world of exam practice. This book will help you get a bit of practice at the kind of questions they're going to throw at you in the exam. It'll also help you to figure out what you need to revise — try answering the questions for the topics you've learnt in class, and if there are any questions that you can't answer then go back and revise that topic some more.

You'll have to do Three Exams

GCSE Edexcel Geography B is divided into three components:
- Global Geographical Issues
- UK Geographical Issues
- People and Environment Issues — Making Geographical Decisions

You'll have to do three exams — one on each of the three components.
Geographical skills will be assessed in all three exams, but fieldwork will only be assessed in Paper 2.
All your exams will take place at the end of the course.

Paper 1: Global Geographical Issues

Paper 1 is divided into three sections.
- Section A covers Hazardous Earth.
- Section B covers Development Dynamics.
- Section C covers Challenges of an Urbanising World.

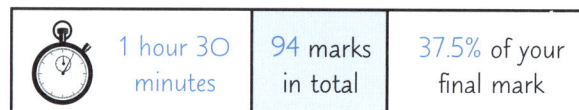

1 hour 30 minutes | 94 marks in total | 37.5% of your final mark

Paper 2: UK Geographical Issues

Paper 2 is divided into three sections.
- Section A covers The UK's Evolving Physical Landscape.
- Section B covers The UK's Evolving Human Landscape.

Section C is split into two parts (C1 and C2). Both parts cover Geographical Investigations:
- C1 covers physical geography fieldwork (Coastal Change and Conflict and River Processes and Pressures).
- C2 covers human geography fieldwork (Dynamic Urban Areas and Changing Rural Areas).

You need to answer all the questions in Sections A and B.
In Section C, make sure you only answer questions on the fieldwork you carried out.

1 hour 30 minutes | 94 marks in total | 37.5% of your final mark

Paper 3: People and Environment Issues — Making Geographical Decisions

In the exam, you'll get a Resource Booklet with lots of information about a geographical issue.
All the questions on Paper 3 will be based on these resources.
Paper 3 is split into four sections.
- Section A covers People and the Biosphere.
- Section B covers Forests Under Threat.
- Section C covers Consuming Energy Resources.

Section D is a decision-making exercise, where you will have to use the sources you have been given and your own knowledge to come to a justified decision about the issue.

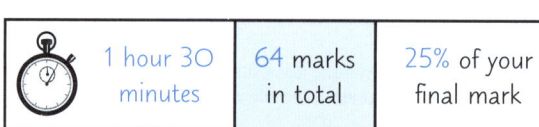

1 hour 30 minutes | 64 marks in total | 25% of your final mark

In each exam, there will be one question which has 4 extra marks available for spelling, punctuation and grammar as well as the use of specialist terminology.
These marks are included in the total marks given for each paper.

Getting Started

Answering Questions

Geography exams would be lovely if it wasn't for those inconvenient questions. A nice couple of hours of peace and quiet to just sit and let your mind wander... Unfortunately, daydreaming about your summer holiday don't butter no parsnips. So here's CGP's top guide to tackling those pesky questions.

Make Sure you Read the Question Properly

It's dead easy to misread the question and spend five minutes writing about the wrong thing.
Four simple tips can help you avoid this:

1) Figure out if it's a case study question — if the question wording includes 'using named examples' or 'for a named country' you need to include a case study or an example you've learnt about.

2) Underline the command words in the question (the ones that tell you what to do):

Command word	Means...
Identify, State or Name	Just give the information you're asked for. You don't need to give any reasons.
Calculate	Do some maths (yikes). Make sure you show your working to get full marks.
Describe	Write about what something is like or what the process involves. You don't need to give reasons but you should try to give as much detail as possible.
Explain	Write about how or why something happens (i.e. give reasons).
Compare	Write about the similarities AND differences.
Suggest	Write about how or why something might happen (i.e. give reasons), applying your knowledge to an unfamiliar situation.
Assess	Weigh up all the factors involved and decide how significant something (e.g. a statement or a cause) is.
Evaluate	Write about how successful something is, including both pros and cons. Make sure you come to a conclusion.
Select and Justify	Pick an option and give reasons why you chose it. Write about why the other options are less suitable as well as why the one you chose is the best.

Answers to questions with 'explain' in them often include the word 'because' (or 'due to').

When writing about differences, 'whereas' is a good word to use in your answers.

3) Underline the key words (the ones that tell you what it's about), e.g. volcanoes, immigration, energy supply.

4) If the question says 'using Figure 2', bloomin' well make sure you've talked about what Figure 2 shows. Don't just wheel out all of your geographical knowledge and forget all about the photo you're supposed to be talking about. Re-read the question and your answer when you've finished, just to check.

Some Questions are Level Marked

Questions worth 8 marks or more with longer written answers are level marked, which means you need to do these things to get the top level and a high mark:

1) Read the question properly and figure out a structure for your answer before you start. Your answer needs to be well organised and structured, and written in a logical way.

2) If it's a case study question, include plenty of relevant details:

> - This includes things like place names, dates, statistics, names of organisations or companies.
> - Don't forget that they need to be relevant though — it's no good including the exact number of people killed in a flood when the question is about the causes of a flood.

3) Some questions have 4 extra marks available for spelling, punctuation and grammar. To get top marks you need to:

- Make sure your spelling, punctuation and grammar are consistently correct.
- Write in a way that makes it clear what you mean.
- Use a wide range of geographical terms (e.g. informal employment) correctly.

Getting Started

Topic 1 — Hazardous Earth

Global Atmospheric Circulation

1 Study **Figure 1**, a map of the world showing bands of high and low pressure and surface winds.

Figure 1

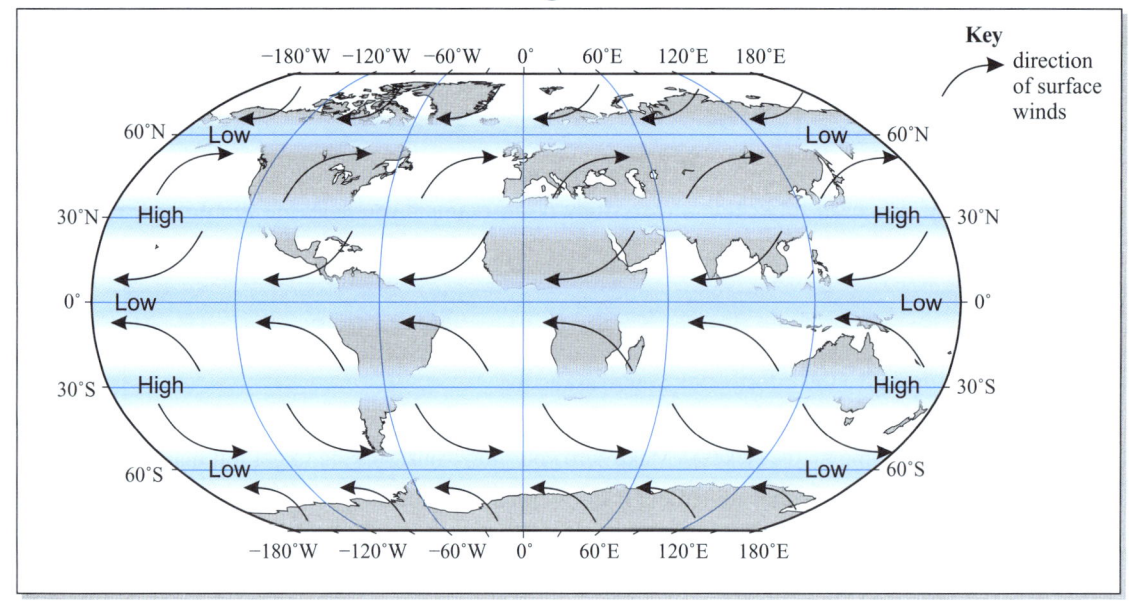

a) Which of the statements below best describes the movement of air at the equator?

- **A** Air rises up. ○
- **B** Air sinks down. ○
- **C** Air moves up and down. ○
- **D** Air is still and does not move. ○

[1]

b) Which of the following descriptions matches the normal weather conditions at a high pressure belt?

- **A** Low rainfall, often cloudy. ○
- **B** High rainfall, often cloudy. ○
- **C** Low rainfall, rarely cloudy. ○
- **D** High rainfall, rarely cloudy. ○

[1]

c) Identify the latitude which receives the most solar radiation.

....
[1]

d) Explain how atmospheric circulation distributes heat energy from the equator to the poles.

....

....

....

....
[4]

[Total 7 marks]

Global Atmospheric Circulation

2 Study **Figure 2**, a map of climatic zones.

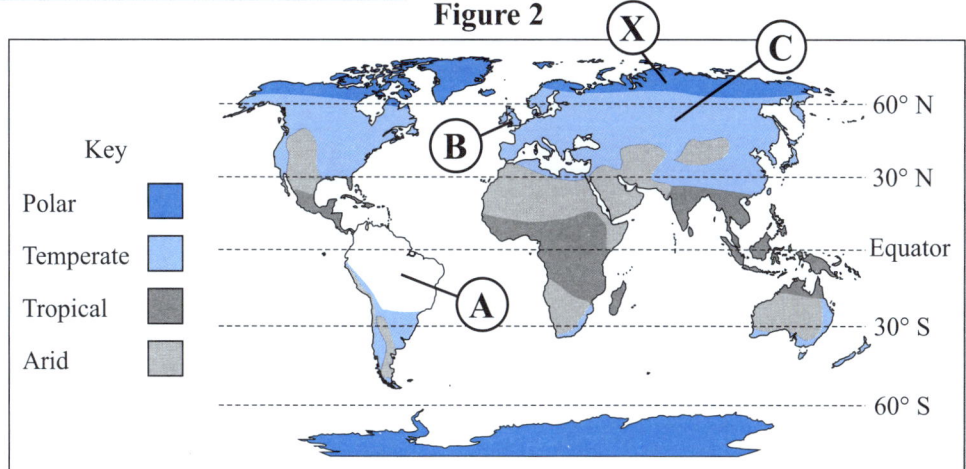

Figure 2

a) **Figure 2** is incomplete. Which climatic zone is found at the location labelled A in **Figure 2**?

  A Polar ○
  B Temperate ○
  C Tropical ○
  D Arid ○

  [1]

b) The average annual temperature at B is 11 °C, but is less than 1 °C at C.
Suggest **one** reason for the difference in temperature between B and C.

  ....
  ....
  ....
  [2]

c) Explain why arid areas are often found around 30° from the equator.

  ....
  ....
  ....
  [2]

d) Suggest the likely climate of the place marked X on **Figure 2**. Give reasons for your answer.

  ....
  ....
  ....
  ....
  ....
  [4]

  [Total 9 marks]

Topic 1 — Hazardous Earth

Natural Climate Change

1 Study **Figure 1**, a graph showing temperature changes during the Quaternary period.

a) Describe the general trends shown in **Figure 1**.

....
....
....
....
....
....
....
[2]

Figure 1

Temperature change in the Antarctic over the last 400 000 years

b) The temperature changes shown in **Figure 1** were worked out from ice core records. Explain how ice cores are used to reconstruct glacial and interglacial climates during the Quaternary period.

....
....
....
[2]

c) Explain **two** possible causes of the changes in temperature between 400 000 and 100 000 years ago shown in **Figure 1**.

1:..

....

....

2:..

....

....
[4]

d) The Little Ice Age was a period of cooling that began about 700 years ago in the UK. Suggest **two** sources of evidence that scientists may have used to reconstruct the climate of this period.

....
....
....
....
....
[4]

[Total 12 marks]

Topic 1 — Hazardous Earth

Climate Change — Human Activity

1 Study **Figure 1**, which shows the average area of sea ice in the Arctic in September between 1979 and 2016.

a) How much did the area of sea ice decrease by between 1980 and 2015?

....
[1]

b) Describe the change in the average area of Arctic sea ice shown by the graph.

....
....
....
....
....
[3]

Figure 1

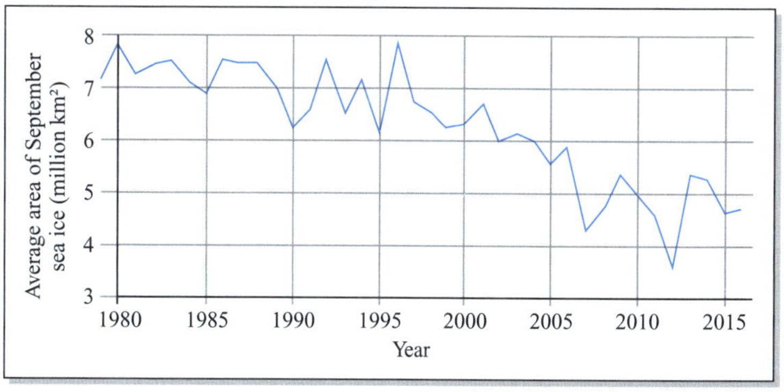

Average area of September sea ice (million km²) vs Year (1980–2015)

Figure 2

Sea level change (cm) vs Year (1900–2100)

Key
— Recorded rise in sea level   -- Max. predicted rise
— Average predicted rise   ····· Min. predicted rise

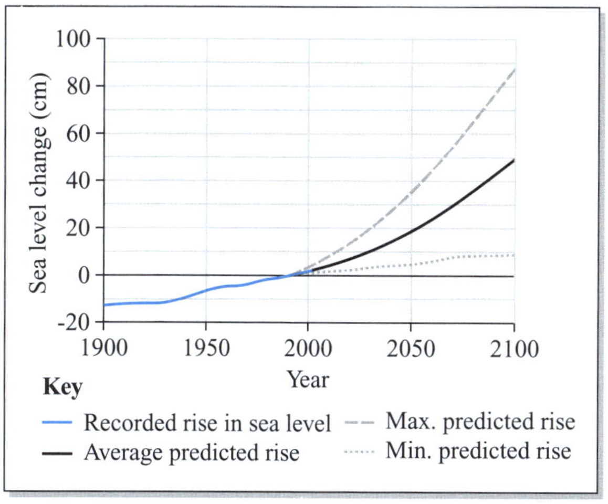

c) Study **Figure 2**, which shows data on sea level rise between 1900 and 2100. Explain how sea level rise provides evidence for global warming.

....
....
....
....
....
....
[2]

d) Suggest **two** reasons for the range in the predictions for sea level rise shown in **Figure 2**.

....
....
....
....
....
[4]

e) 'Past climate change helps scientists to predict how climate will change in the future.'
Assess this statement.

[8]

[Total 18 marks]

Topic 1 — Hazardous Earth

Climate Change — Human Activity

2 Study **Figure 3**, a photograph of a coal-fired power plant in South Africa.

a) Explain what impact this activity may have on climate change.

Figure 3

....
....
....
....
....
....
....
[4]

b) Explain how **one** other human activity may contribute to climate change.

....
....
....
[2]
[Total 6 marks]

3 Study **Figure 4**, which shows the maize yield and annual rainfall for a low latitude farm in Central Africa.

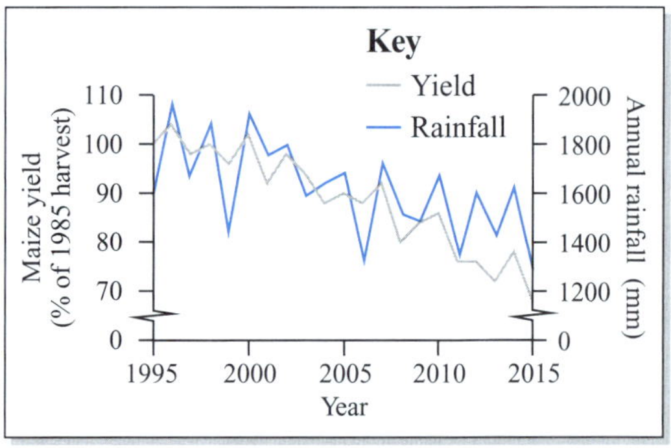

a) Using **Figure 4**, describe how climate change may be affecting crop yields in low latitude areas.

Figure 4

....
....
....
....
[2]

b) Suggest **one** possible effect on people of the trends in crop yield shown in **Figure 4**.

....
....
[2]

c) Identify **one** effect, other than changing crop yields, that climate change may have on people.

....
[1]
[Total 5 marks]

Topic 1 — Hazardous Earth

Tropical Cyclones

1 Study **Figure 1**, a map showing the areas affected by tropical cyclones.

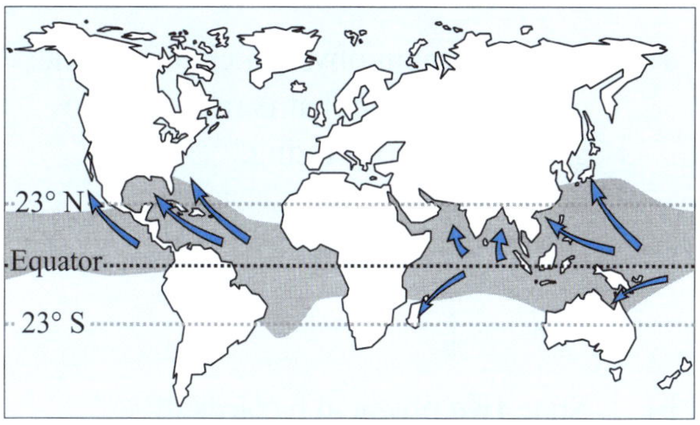

a) Using **Figure 1**, explain the global distribution of tropical cyclones.

....
....
....
....
....
....
[2]

Figure 1

[Map showing tropical cyclone paths between 23°N and 23°S, with key: arrow = path of tropical cyclone; shaded area = sea surface temperature 26.5 °C or higher]

b) Explain the seasonal distribution of tropical cyclones in the northern hemisphere.

....
....
....
[2]

c) State **two** features of tropical cyclones.

1: ....

2: ....
[2]

d) Which of the following would cause a tropical cyclone to intensify?

    A   The cyclone moving over land.   ◯

    B   The cyclone meeting another weather system.   ◯

    C   The cyclone moving over warmer water.   ◯

    D   The cyclone changing direction.   ◯
[1]

e) Explain how the global circulation of the atmosphere affects the track of tropical cyclones.

....
....
....
....
....
[4]

[Total 11 marks]

Topic 1 — Hazardous Earth

Tropical Cyclones — Impacts

1   Study **Figure 1**, a photograph of Slidell, Louisiana after Hurricane Katrina in 2005. Hurricane Katrina had a Category 3 rating on the Saffir-Simpson Scale when it made landfall.

a) State the main physical characteristic of the hurricane that is measured to give its category rating.

....
[1]

Figure 1

b) State **two** physical hazards of tropical cyclones.

1:..

....

2:..
[2]

c) Using **Figure 1**, identify **two** ways that tropical cyclones impact people.

1:..

2:..
[2]

d) Explain **one** longer-term impact on people that may result from a tropical cyclone.

....

....

....
[2]

e) Describe **two** impacts that tropical cyclones can have on the environment.

1:..

....

....

2:..

....

....
[4]

[Total 11 marks]

Topic 1 — Hazardous Earth

Tropical Cyclones — Preparation and Responses

1 Study **Figure 1**, a forecast map showing the predicted path of a hurricane over Cuba, approaching Miami, Florida.

Figure 1

a) Which of the following is **not** used to work out the predicted paths of cyclones?

   A   Seismometers ◯
   B   Satellite photos ◯
   C   Computer models ◯
   D   Weather forecasting technology ◯
   [1]

b) Explain how this prediction could help to reduce the effects of the cyclone in Miami.

   ....
   ....
   ....
   [2]

c) Explain how cities such as Miami could defend themselves to reduce the impacts of tropical cyclones.

   ....
   ....
   ....
   ....
   ....
   [4]

d) Explain **one** way a country can be physically vulnerable to the impacts of tropical cyclones.

   ....
   ....
   ....
   [2]

e) Compare the vulnerability of developed and developing countries to the impacts of tropical cyclones.

   ....
   ....
   ....
   ....
   [3]

f) Referring to **two** countries with contrasting levels of development, assess the effectiveness of the preparation methods used in reducing the impacts of tropical cyclones.
   [8]

[Total 20 marks]

Structure of the Earth

1 Study **Figure 1**, a diagram showing the Earth's structure.

Figure 1

a) What feature is labelled A in **Figure 1**?

   A Crust ◯
   B Plate boundary ◯
   C Mantle ◯
   D Magma ◯

   [1]

b) Name and describe the feature labelled B in **Figure 1**.

   ....
   ....
   ....
   [2]

c) Which statement below best describes the difference between the inner core and the outer core?

   A The inner core is liquid; the outer core is solid. ◯
   B The inner core is solid; the outer core is liquid. ◯
   C The outer core is divided into tectonic plates; the inner core is not. ◯
   D The inner core is divided into tectonic plates; the outer core is not. ◯

   [1]

d) Describe how continental crust is different from oceanic crust.

   ....
   ....
   ....
   [2]

e) Explain how convection currents cause tectonic plates to move.

   ....
   ....
   ....
   ....
   ....
   ....
   [4]

   [Total 10 marks]

Topic 1 — Hazardous Earth

Plate Boundaries

1   Study **Figure 1**, which shows the Earth's tectonic plates.

Figure 1

a) Name the type of plate boundary labelled A in **Figure 1** and explain why new crust forms there.

    ....

    ....

    ....

    ....

    ....

    ....
    [3]

b) Name the type of plate boundary found at the location labelled B on **Figure 1**.

    ....
    [1]

c) State **two** ways that tectonic plates could move in relation to each other at the type of plate boundary you identified in b).

    ....

    ....

    ....
    [2]

d) Study **Figure 2**, which is a diagram of a plate boundary. Name the type of plate boundary shown.

    ....
    [1]

Figure 2

e) State what happens when **two continental** plates meet at the type of plate boundary shown in **Figure 2**.

    ....

    ....

    ....

    ....

    ....
    [1]

    [Total 8 marks]

Topic 1 — Hazardous Earth

Volcanic Hazards

1   Study **Figure 1**, which shows the Earth's tectonic plates and the distribution of volcanoes.

a) Name the type of plate boundary labelled A in **Figure 1** and explain how volcanoes are formed at this location.

....
....
....
....
....
....
....
[4]

b) Hawaii is labelled B on **Figure 1**. There are volcanoes in Hawaii, even though it is in the centre of a tectonic plate. Explain how volcanoes form away from plate boundaries.

....
....
....
....
[3]

[Total 7 marks]

2   Study **Figure 2**, which shows a cross-section through a shield volcano.

a) Explain how the volcano gets its characteristic shape.

....
....
....
....
[2]

b) Compare the characteristics of shield volcanoes and composite volcanoes.

....
....
....
....
[3]

[Total 5 marks]

Topic 1 — Hazardous Earth

Earthquake Hazards

1 Study **Figure 1**, which shows the Earth's tectonic plates and the distribution of earthquakes.

Figure 1

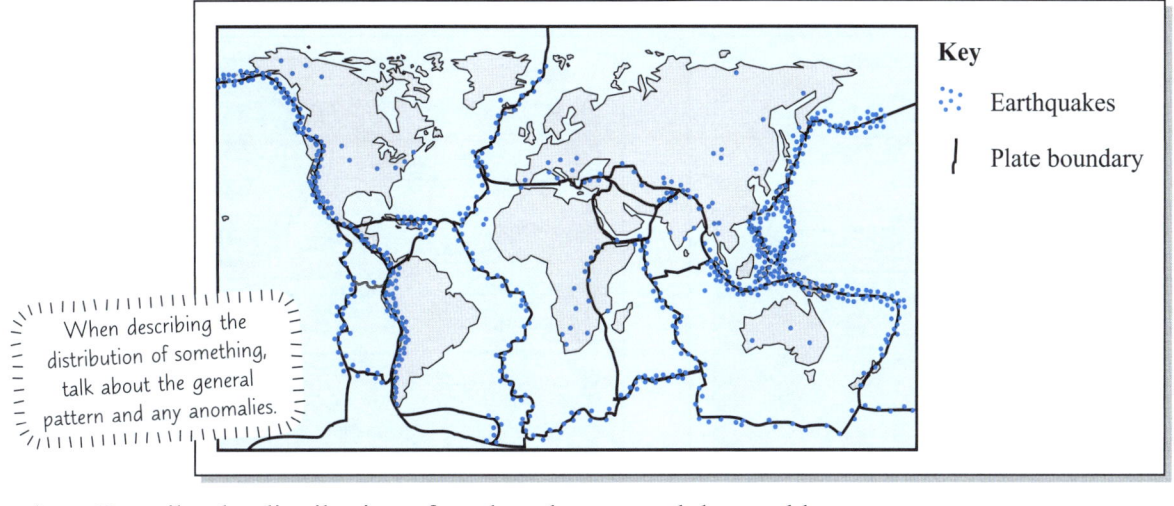

When describing the distribution of something, talk about the general pattern and any anomalies.

a) Describe the distribution of earthquakes around the world.

....
....
....
[2]

b) Explain how earthquakes are caused at convergent plate boundaries.

....
....
....
....
[3]

c) Which of the following best describes deep-focus earthquakes?

    A   They do more damage than shallow-focus earthquakes. ◯

    B   Their focus is on or near the Earth's surface. ◯

    C   They have a lower magnitude than shallow-focus earthquakes. ◯

    D   They are caused by subducted crust moving towards the centre of the Earth. ◯
[1]

d) Explain how shallow-focus earthquakes cause tsunamis.

....
....
....
[2]

[Total 8 marks]

Topic 1 — Hazardous Earth

Impacts of Tectonic Hazards

1   Study **Figure 1**, which shows some of the effects of a volcanic eruption in Montserrat in 1997, and **Figure 2**, which shows some of the effects of an earthquake in Nepal in 2015.

Figure 1

Figure 2

a)   Using **Figure 1** or **Figure 2** and your own knowledge, identify **two** primary effects of **either** volcanic eruptions **or** earthquakes. Tick the circle of the hazard you have chosen.

Volcanic eruptions ◯   Earthquakes ◯

Effect 1:..

....

Effect 2:..

....
[2]

b)   Using **Figure 1** or **Figure 2** and your own knowledge, identify **two** secondary effects of **either** volcanic eruptions **or** earthquakes. Tick the circle of the hazard you have chosen.

Volcanic eruptions ◯   Earthquakes ◯

Effect 1:..

....

Effect 2:..

....
[2]

c)   Suggest why the effects of a tectonic hazard may be greater in a urban location than a rural one.

....

....

....
[2]

[Total 6 marks]

Topic 1 — Hazardous Earth

Management of Tectonic Hazards

1   **Figure 1** shows the effects of **two** tectonic hazards in different parts of the world. One occurred in a developing country and one occurred in a developed country.

a)   Using evidence from **Figure 1**, suggest which hazard took place in a developing country. Give a reason for your answer.

Figure 1

	Hazard A	Hazard B
Number of deaths in first 24 hours after event	9084	208
Number of deaths in first 30 days after event	19 790	221
Cost of rebuilding (US$)	4 billion	16 billion

....

....

....

....

....
[2]

b)   Calculate the ratio of the cost of rebuilding after Hazard A to the cost of rebuilding after Hazard B.

....
[1]

c)   Give **two** ways that short-term relief could have reduced the number of deaths caused by Hazard A.

1:..

....

2:..

....
[2]

d)   Scientists monitor gases and ground vibrations in tectonically active areas. Explain how this helps them to predict tectonic hazards.

....

....

....
[2]

e)   'Preparation reduces the impact of tectonic hazards.' Assess this statement using examples of hazards in countries of contrasting levels of development.

[8 + 4 SPaG]

[Total 19 marks]

Measuring Development

1   Study **Figure 1**, which shows measures of development for Canada, Malaysia and Angola.

a) Identify which of the following is a measure of economic development.

A   GNI per capita   ○

B   Birth rate   ○

C   Life expectancy   ○

D   Literacy rate   ○   [1]

Figure 1

	Canada	Malaysia	Angola
GNI per capita	$51 770	$11 120	$4800
Birth rate	10.28	19.71	38.78
Death rate	8.42	5.03	11.49
Infant mortality rate	4.65	13.27	78.26
Life expectancy	81.76	74.75	55.63
Literacy rate	97.1%	94.6%	71.1%
HDI value	0.913	0.779	0.532

b) Define birth rate.

....

[1]

c) Explain how the differences in birth rates shown in **Figure 1** could be a consequence of differences in the level of development.

....

....

....

[2]

d) State what is meant by the Gross National Income (GNI) per capita of a country.

....

....

[1]

e) Explain why the Human Development Index (HDI) values given in **Figure 1** may be a better measure of development than any of the other measures.

....

....

....

[2]

f) Explain **one** political indicator that can be used to determine the level of development in a country.

....

....

....

....

[3]

Measuring Development

g) Explain which of the countries shown in **Figure 1** is the most developed.

....
....
....
....
....
....

[4]

[Total 14 marks]

2 Study **Figure 2**, which shows population pyramids for countries A, B and C.

Figure 2

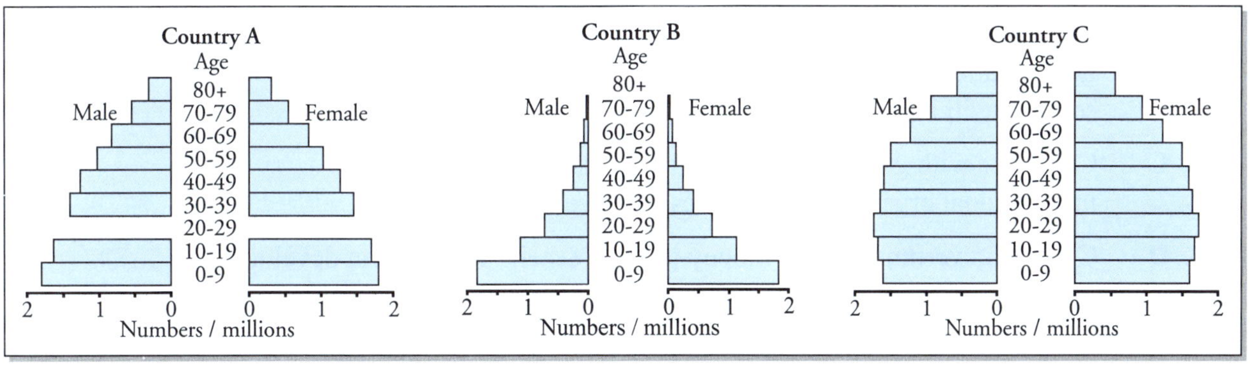

a) Complete **Figure 2** to show that the population of Country A includes 1.6 million women aged 20-29, and 1.5 million men aged 20-29.

[1]

b) Compare the population pyramids for Country A and Country B.

....
....
....
....

[3]

c) Explain whether Country C is developing, emerging or developed.

....
....
....
....

[3]

[Total 7 marks]

Topic 2 — Development Dynamics

Global Inequalities

1 Study **Figure 1**, an article about Libya written in 2016.

Figure 1

Libya is the fourth largest country in Africa. It's located on the northern edge of the Sahara desert. More than 90% of the country is a desert or semi-desert environment.

Libya was an Italian colony for much of the early 20th century until it was captured and occupied by Allied forces during the Second World War. Libya declared independence in December 1951.

Since gaining independence, Libya has suffered from periods of poor international relations and conflict. It currently has a medium level of development.

a) Which of the following statements about political influences on development is true?

    A Authoritarian governments often have better international relations, increasing development. ◯

    B Democratic governments usually have poor trade links, so there will be less money to spend on development. ◯

    C Countries with good international relations can get loans from international organisations to invest in development projects. ◯

    D Corrupt governments take money that isn't theirs to spend on development. ◯

[1]

b) Explain how being a former colony may affect a country's economic development.

....

....

....

....

[3]

c) Using **Figure 1**, explain how climate may have affected the level of development of Libya.

....

....

....

....

....

[4]

d) State **one** other physical factor that can affect how developed a country is.

....

[1]

[Total 9 marks]

Topic 2 — Development Dynamics

Global Inequalities

2   Study **Figure 2**, which shows the highest level of education achieved by people aged 21 and over in countries A and B.

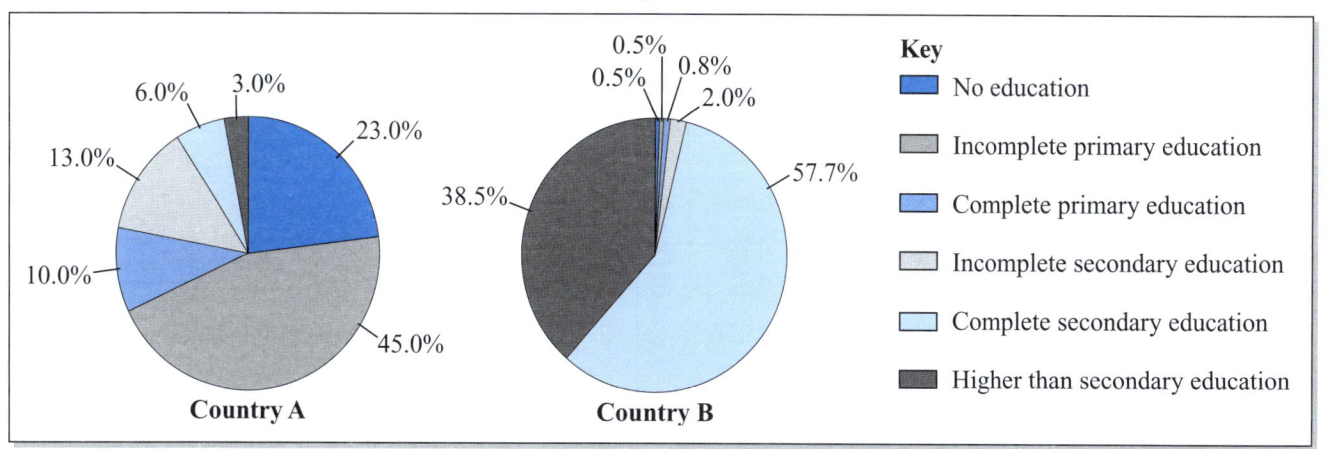

Figure 2

a) State the percentage of people aged 21 and over in Country A who are educated beyond secondary level.

    ....
    [1]

b) In 2016, the population of Country B was 8.2 million. Using **Figure 2**, calculate the number of people aged 21 and over whose highest level of education is a complete secondary education.

    ....
    [2]

c) Using **Figure 2**, explain which country is most likely to be more developed.

    ....
    ....
    ....
    [2]

d) Explain the likely differences between the health of people in Country A and Country B.

    ....
    ....
    ....
    ....
    [3]

e) Explain **one** possible difference between the level of localised pollution likely to be found in Country A and Country B.

    ....
    ....
    ....
    [2]

[Total 10 marks]

Topic 2 — Development Dynamics

Theories of Development

1 Study **Figure 1**, which shows Rostow's modernisation theory of the stages of economic development.

a) Which of the following features is a defining characteristic of Stage 3 of Rostow's modernisation theory?

  A Widespread use of technology. ○

  B Subsistence farming. ○

  C Manufacturing starts to develop. ○

  D Large-scale industrialisation. ○

[1]

Figure 1

Graph showing Level of Development against Time, with Stage 1: Traditional society, Stage 2: Preconditions for take-off, Stage 3: Take-off, Stage 4: Drive to maturity, Stage 5: Mass consumption.

b) Which statement best describes Stage 4 of Rostow's modernisation theory?

  A Manufacturing industries begin to develop, along with the infrastructure needed to support them. ○

  B The population becomes increasingly wealthy, the use of technology increases and standards of living rise. ○

  C The economy is largely subsistence-based and there is very little international trade. ○

  D Goods are mass produced, and the wealthy population means that levels of consumption are very high. ○

[1]

c) Frank's dependency theory suggests that neo-colonialism is holding development back in some countries. What is meant by 'neo-colonialism'?

....

....

[1]

d) Explain why neo-colonialism may hinder development according to Frank's dependency theory.

....

....

....

....

....

[4]

[Total 7 marks]

Topic 2 — Development Dynamics

Globalisation

1 Improvements in air transport are partly responsible for the increase in globalisation.
Study **Figure 1**, which shows the number of passengers using UK airports from 1960 to 2015.

a) Define the term 'globalisation'.

....

....

....

....

....

....
[1]

Figure 1

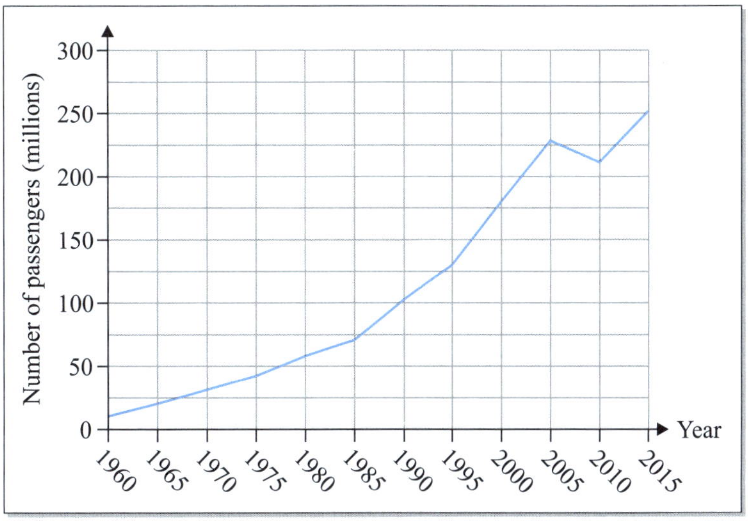

[Graph: Number of passengers (millions) vs Year, showing increase from ~10 million in 1960 to ~250 million in 2015]

b) Using **Figure 1**, calculate the difference between the number of passengers using UK airports in 1960 and in 2000.

....
[1]

c) Suggest how improvements in air travel have increased globalisation.

....

....

....
[2]

d) Explain how transnational corporations (TNCs) increase globalisation.

....

....

....
[2]

e) State **two** ways that governments can increase globalisation.

1:..

2:..
[2]

f) Some countries have grown rapidly wealthier as a result of globalisation. State **two** conditions that may have given them an advantage over other countries that have not developed as rapidly.

1:..

2:..
[2]

[Total 10 marks]

Reducing Global Inequalities

1 Development strategies can help to reduce global inequalities. These strategies can be described as 'top-down' or 'bottom-up'.

a) Which of the following statements best describes 'bottom-up' development strategies?

   A   Strategies where transnational corporations direct projects designed to increase development with little or no input from local communities. ○

   B   Strategies which usually use high-tech equipment and machinery, often operated by skilled workers from developed countries. ○

   C   Strategies funded by governments or companies to aid development with the aim of generating profit. ○

   D   Strategies where local people and communities decide on ways to improve things for their own community. ○

   [1]

b) Development strategies are often led by NGOs. What is an NGO?

   ....
   [1]

c) State **one** advantage of development strategies being led by NGOs.

   ....
   ....
   [1]

d) Large-scale infrastructure projects may be funded by inter-governmental organisations (IGOs) or transnational corporations (TNCs). Compare the benefits for the recipient country of infrastructure projects funded by IGOs or TNCs.

   ....
   ....
   ....
   ....
   [3]

e) Explain the disadvantages of 'top-down' strategies for the recipient country.

   ....
   ....
   ....
   ....
   ....
   [4]

   [Total 10 marks]

Development in Emerging Countries

1 Study **Figure 1**, which shows the contributions of primary industry, secondary industry and services to the total GDP of an emerging country.

Figure 1

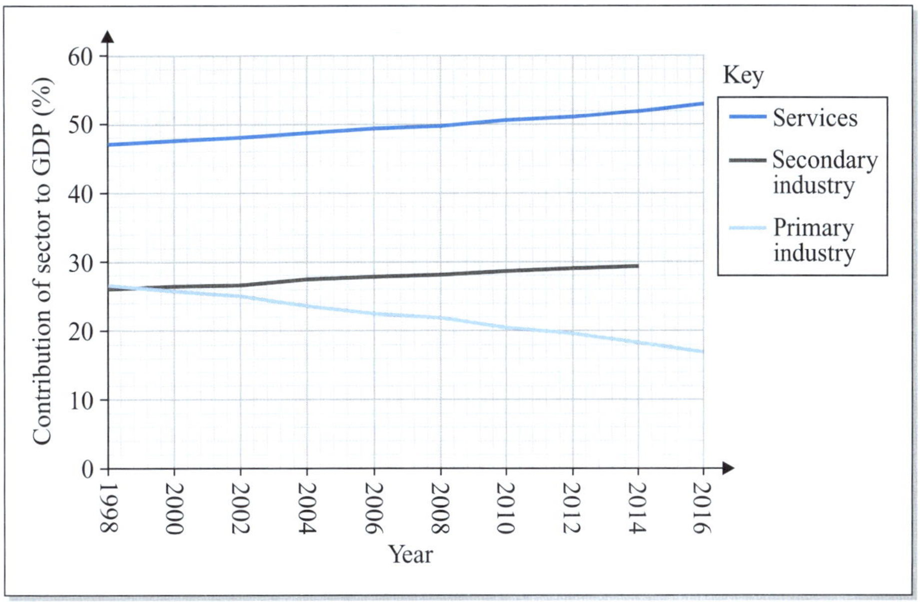

a) Complete **Figure 1** to show that secondary industry contributed 30% to the total GDP in 2016.
[1]

b) The country's total GDP in 2016 was US$ 1.9 trillion.
Calculate the amount of GDP contributed by primary industry in 2016 in US$.

....
[2]

c) Using **Figure 1**, give **one** piece of evidence that suggests that the data is from an emerging country.

....

....
[1]

d) For an emerging country you have studied, explain the changes to imports and exports since 1990.

....

....

....

....

....
[4]

[Total 8 marks]

Topic 2 — Development Dynamics

Development in Emerging Countries

2 Study **Figure 2**, which shows development data for four different regions of an emerging country. Two of the regions are urban and two are rural.

Figure 2

Region	A	B	C	D
Infant mortality rate (per 1000 live births)	34	15	11	31
Literacy rate (%)	63	87	91	69
GDP per capita (US$)	686	2201	2507	798

a) Which **two** of the regions are most likely to be rural?

- **A** A and D ○
- **B** A and B ○
- **C** B and C ○
- **D** B and D ○

[1]

b) Suggest **one** reason for the regional variation in GDP per capita.

....

....

....
[2]

c) Suggest why literacy rate varies between the regions in **Figure 2**.

....

....

....
[2]

d) Economic development can cause changes to population structure. For an emerging country that you have studied, explain how the population structure has changed as the country has developed.

....

....

....

....

....
[4]

e) Evaluate the positive and negative impacts of economic development on different groups of people in an emerging country that you have studied.

[8 + 4 SPaG]

[Total 21 marks]

Topic 2 — Development Dynamics

Development in Emerging Countries

3   Study **Figure 3**, which shows the yearly level of foreign direct investment (FDI) in a region of an emerging country between 2008 and 2016.

Figure 3

a)   Using **Figure 3**, describe how FDI in the region changed between 2008 and 2016.

   ....
   ....
   ....
   [2]

b)   Explain **one** negative impact of FDI for an emerging country.

   ....
   ....
   ....
   [2]

c)   For a named emerging country, explain **one** way that government policy on FDI has affected the country's development.

   ....
   ....
   ....
   [2]

d)   Explain **two** other ways in which government policy has increased development in an emerging country you have studied.

   1: ....
   ....
   2: ....
   ....
   [4]

e)   'The increasing geopolitical influence of emerging countries is a positive change.'
     Assess this statement, using specific examples from a country that you have studied.
     [8 + 4 SPaG]

   [Total 22 marks]

Topic 3 — Challenges of an Urbanising World

Urbanisation

1 Study **Figure 1**, a graph showing the change in the urban population of more developed countries and less developed countries between 1950 and 2000.

a) Complete the graph to show that the urban population of less developed countries in 2000 was 2 billion.
[1]

b) Describe the trends shown in **Figure 1**.

....

....

....

....

....

....
[3]
[Total 4 marks]

2 Study **Figure 2**, which shows the global distribution of megacities in 1975 and 2014.

a) Describe the changes in the number and distribution of megacities between 1975 and 2014 shown in **Figure 2**.

....

....

....

....

....

....
[3]

b) What is meant by the term 'primate city'?

....
[1]

c) Which of the following is **not** a common characteristic of primate cities?

- A   They have low rates of migration.   ○
- B   International ports and airports are located there.   ○
- C   Large, powerful businesses influence their development.   ○
- D   They are centres for trade and business.   ○

[1]
[Total 5 marks]

Cities — Growth and Decline

1 Study the table showing the rural and urban populations of the Republic of the Congo in 1990 and 2014.

Figure 1

	Rural	Urban
1990	1100	1300
2014	1600	3000

Population in thousands

a) Calculate the ratio of the rural to urban population in the Republic of the Congo in 2014. Give your answer in its simplest form.

....

....
[1]

b) Which of the following best describes how economic change in emerging countries is affecting the proportion of people living in urban areas?

    A   Most cities have declining populations. ◯

    B   Some cities have stable populations and others are declining. ◯

    C   Most cities have stable populations. ◯

    D   Some cities are growing and some have stabilising populations. ◯

[1]

c) Give **two** push factors that encourage people to move from rural areas to cities.

1:..

2:..
[2]

d) Explain how economic change in developing countries is having an effect on national migration.

....

....

....

....

....
[4]

e) Suggest **two** reasons why the rate of urbanisation is different in developing and developed countries.

1:..

....

....

2:..

....

....
[4]

[Total 12 marks]

Urban Economies

1 Study **Figure 1**, which shows the employment structure of an urban area in 2016.

a) What is meant by the term 'tertiary industry'?

....

....
[1]

b) Suggest whether the urban area in **Figure 1** is in a developed or developing country. Give a reason for your answer.

....

....

....

....

....
[2]

c) Describe how the proportion of people working in the informal sector changes as a country develops.

....

....

....
[2]

d) Which of the following is **not** likely to be a challenge faced by a worker in the informal sector?

    A   Working in dangerous conditions.   ◯

    B   Working long hours.   ◯

    C   Earning very little.   ◯

    D   Having to pay high taxes.   ◯
[1]

e) Explain why the proportion of people working in the secondary sector changes as a country develops.

....

....

....

....
[4]

[Total 10 marks]

Urban Change

1 Suburbanisation is influenced by a range of factors.

a) Define the term 'suburbanisation'.

....
[1]

b) Which **one** of the following is **not** a factor leading to suburbanisation?

    A   Planning laws outside the city centre are relaxed, so it's easier to build houses. ◯

    B   Suburban areas have more green spaces, so quality of life is higher. ◯

    C   Public transport is often good in suburban areas, so commuting is easy. ◯

    D   Suburban areas have many nightclubs and bars, so entertainment is easily accessible. ◯
[1]

[Total 2 marks]

2 Study **Figure 1**, a table showing the population change and business start-ups in four UK urban areas between 2004 and 2014.

Figure 1

a) Using **Figure 1**, which city is most likely to be undergoing regeneration?

    A   Bournemouth ◯

    B   Wigan ◯

    C   Swansea ◯

    D   Sunderland ◯
[1]

	Population change (2004-2014)	Business start-ups 2014 (per 10 000 of population)
Bournemouth	10.17%	51.30
Wigan	5.25%	37.23
Swansea	4.52%	32.48
Sunderland	-1.14%	30.16

b) State **two** ways that urban areas are affected by de-industrialisation.

1: ....

2: ....
[2]

c) Explain the strategies that can be used to regenerate city centres in developed countries.

....

....

....

....

....
[4]

[Total 7 marks]

Topic 3 — Challenges of an Urbanising World

Urban Land Use

1 Study **Figures 1** and **2**. **Figure 1** is a photograph of part of a city. **Figure 2** is a model of a typical city in a developed country viewed from above, which shows where the **four** different parts of a city are located.

a) Name the type of land use shown in **Figure 1**.

....
[1]

b) Label **Figure 2** with an **X** to show where you would expect the land use shown in **Figure 1** to be found.
[1]

c) State **two** types of land use often found in the zone labelled **A** on **Figure 2**.

1: ....

2: ....
[2]

d) Explain **one** way that planning regulations influence land use in cities.

....

....

....

....
[2]

e) Explain how typical land use on the edge of a city is influenced by accessibility and cost.

....

....

....

....

....
[4]

f) Explain how land use in the centre of cities might change over time.

....

....

....
[2]

[Total 12 marks]

Topic 3 — Challenges of an Urbanising World

Urban Change in Megacities

1 The populations of many megacities in developing and emerging countries are growing rapidly.

a) Which of the following statements is correct?

    A   Megacities have a population of less than 10 000 people. ◯

    B   Megacities have a population of less than 1 million people. ◯

    C   Megacities have a population of more than 10 million people. ◯

    D   Megacities have a population of more than 100 million people. ◯

[1]

b) State **two** locational factors that can influence the growth of a megacity.

1:..

2:..

[2]

c) What is meant by the term 'natural increase'?

....

[1]

d) Explain why the population is growing rapidly in a megacity in an emerging or a developing country you have studied.

....

....

....

....

....

[4]

[Total 8 marks]

2 Study **Figure 1**, a diagram showing land use in a model megacity in an emerging country.

a) Label the diagram in **Figure 1** to show where the oldest buildings are likely to be found.

[1]

b) Identify the part of a city where rapid growth is most likely to be taking place.

....

[1]

c) Identify the part of a city where high density low-quality housing is most likely to be found.

....

[1]

Figure 1

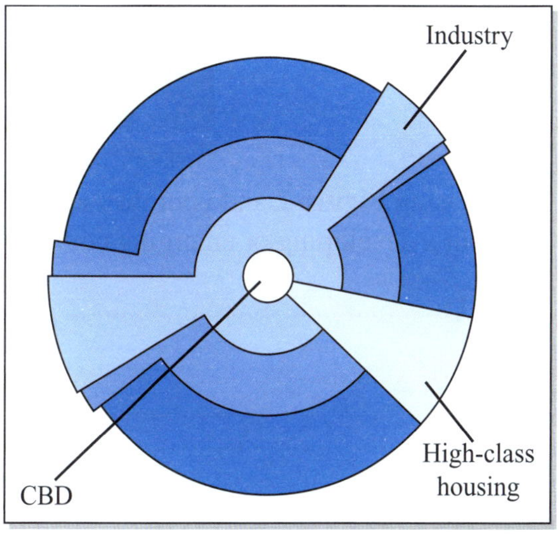

(Diagram showing concentric zones with labels: CBD, Industry, High-class housing)

Topic 3 — Challenges of an Urbanising World

Urban Change in Megacities

d) Suggest **one** reason for the location of industry in **Figure 1**.

....

....

....
[2]

e) Describe **two** ways that rapid population growth has led to a change in land use in a megacity in an emerging or developing country that you have studied.

1:..

....

....

2:..

....

....
[4]

[Total 9 marks]

3   Study **Figure 2**, a photograph of some students in a city in Indonesia, an emerging country.

Figure 2

a) Using **Figure 2** and your own knowledge, state **two** opportunities for people living in a megacity in a developing or emerging country compared to living in rural areas.

1:..

....

2:..

....
[2]

Urban Change in Megacities

b) Suggest why there are big differences in quality of life within megacities in emerging countries.

....

....

....

....

....
[4]

c) Explain how inequalities create challenges for the management of a named megacity.

....

....

....

....

....
[4]

[Total 10 marks]

4 Study **Figure 3**, a photo of a squatter settlement in a megacity in an emerging country.

a) Define the term 'squatter settlement'.

....

....

....
[1]

Figure 3

b) Explain why squatter settlements, like the one shown in **Figure 3**, develop in megacities in developing or emerging countries.

....

....

....

....

....

....
[2]

Topic 3 — Challenges of an Urbanising World

Urban Change in Megacities

c) Explain **two** challenges for people living in squatter settlements.

1:..

....

2:..

....

[4]

[Total 7 marks]

5   Study **Figure 4**, an extract from a website promoting the Can-Can Squatter Settlement Redevelopment Project, a bottom-up strategy being run in a megacity in an emerging country.

Figure 4

The Can-Can Squatter Settlement Redevelopment Project started in 2006 to help improve life for residents of this squatter settlement. The project involves self-help and local authority schemes including the installation of a sewage disposal system. The project also aims to improve quality of life by improving health care and education.

Year	Literacy rate	% people in work	% people with access to clean water	No. of people per doctor	Average life expectancy
1995	3%	27	33	2000	49
2005	3%	26	36	2000	49
2015	37%	69	73	500	57

a) By how much did life expectancy increase between 1995 and 2015?

....

[1]

b) State **one** disadvantage of 'bottom-up strategies' being used in megacities.

....

....

[1]

c) Use evidence from **Figure 4** to describe the success of the Can-Can project.

....

....

....

[2]

d) For a named megacity in an emerging or developing country, assess the effectiveness of top-down and bottom-up strategies that have been used to make it more sustainable.

[8 + 4 SPaG]

[Total 16 marks]

Topic 3 — Challenges of an Urbanising World

Topic 4 — The UK's Evolving Physical Landscape

Rocks and the UK Physical Landscape

1 Study **Figure 1**, a map of the UK's upland and lowland areas.

a) Identify area A in **Figure 1**.

   A The Grampian Mountains in Scotland ○
   B The Pennines in England ○
   C The Lake District in England ○
   D The Cairngorms in Scotland ○

   [1]

Figure 1

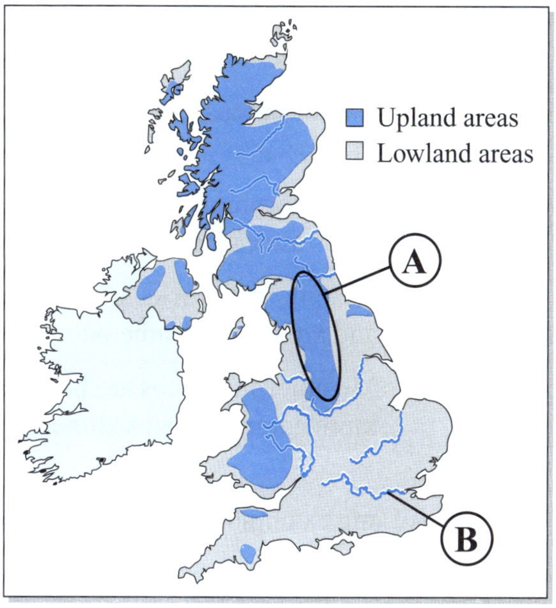

■ Upland areas
□ Lowland areas

b) Identify the feature marked B in **Figure 1**.

   A The River Severn ○
   B The Firth of Forth ○
   C The Bristol Channel ○
   D The River Thames ○

   [1]

c) Describe the physical characteristics of lowland areas in the UK.

   ....
   ....
   ....
   [2]

d) State **two** ways in which past glacial processes have shaped upland areas in the UK.

   1: ....
   2: ....
   [2]

e) Explain how past tectonic processes have shaped the UK landscape.

   ....
   ....
   ....
   ....
   ....
   [4]

   [Total 10 marks]

Rocks and the UK Physical Landscape

2 Study **Figure 2**, which shows the distribution of different rock types in the UK.

a) Which **two** of the following statements are true of metamorphic rocks?

    A All metamorphic rocks are permeable. ◯

    B Carboniferous limestone is an example of a metamorphic rock. ◯

    C Metamorphic rocks are formed when other rocks are changed by heat and pressure. ◯

    D Metamorphic rocks are very soft and are easily weathered. ◯

    E Metamorphic rocks are harder and more compact than sedimentary rocks. ◯

Figure 2

Key
- Igneous rocks
- Sedimentary rocks
- Metamorphic rocks

[2]

b) Give **one** example of a sedimentary rock.

....

[1]

c) Define the term 'igneous rock'.

....

[1]

d) State **one** characteristic of igneous rock.

....

[1]

e) Using **Figure 2**, describe the distribution of igneous rocks in the UK.

....

....

....

[2]

f) Explain how geology has influenced the development of the landscape shown in **Figure 3**.

Figure 3

....

....

....

....

....

....

[2]

[Total 9 marks]

Landscape Processes — Physical

1 Study **Figure 1**, a photo of an area in the Lake District.

Figure 1

a) Identify the landform shown in **Figure 1**.

    A   Glacial trough ○

    B   Tor ○

    C   V-shaped valley ○

    D   Corrie ○

[1]

b) Name **one** type of weathering that may be altering the landscape shown in **Figure 1**.

....
[1]

c) Suggest **two** ways that slope processes may be modifying the landscape shown in **Figure 1**.

1:..

....

2:..

....
[4]

d) Explain **one** way that climate may be influencing the physical processes in this landscape.

....

....

....
[2]

[Total 8 marks]

2 Study **Figure 2**, a photo of a lowland area in the UK.

Figure 2

Explain how the interaction of physical processes may lead to the formation of lowland landscapes such as the one shown in **Figure 2**.

....

....

....

....

....

....

....
[Total 3 marks]

Topic 4 — The UK's Evolving Physical Landscape

Landscape Processes — Human

1 Study **Figure 1**, an Ordnance Survey® map of Thetford, Norfolk, a lowland area in the east of England.

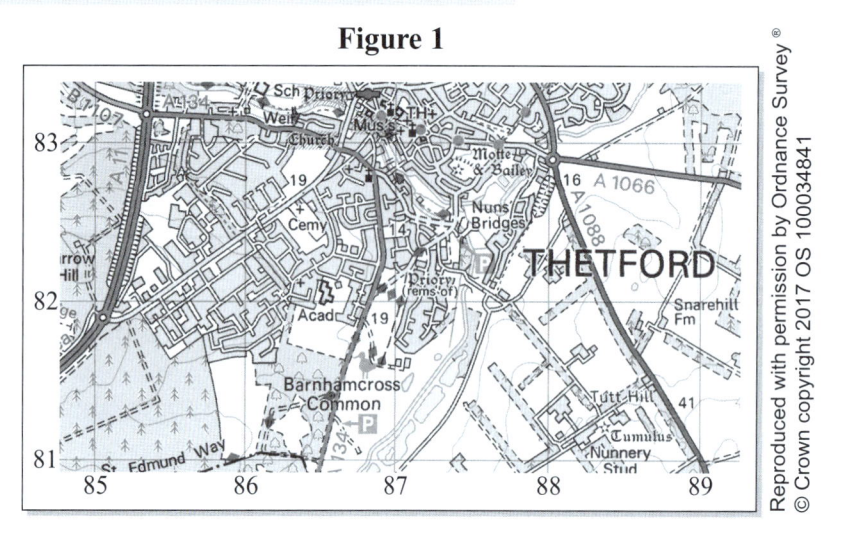

Figure 1

a) Using **Figure 1**, give **one** piece of evidence that agriculture is taking place in this area.

....

....
[1]

b) Using **Figure 1**, identify **two** ways that human settlement has altered the landscape in grid square 8582.

1:..

2:..
[2]

c) Using **Figure 1**, describe **one** way that forestry may be influencing the landscape.

....

....

....
[2]

d) Give two possible reasons why the land surrounding Thetford is suitable for arable farming.

1:..

2:..
[2]

e) Explain how farming in upland areas is different to farming in lowland areas.

....

....

....
[2]

[Total 9 marks]

Coastal Change and Conflict

Coastal Weathering and Erosion

1 Study **Figure 1**, which shows how the coastline of an area has changed over time.

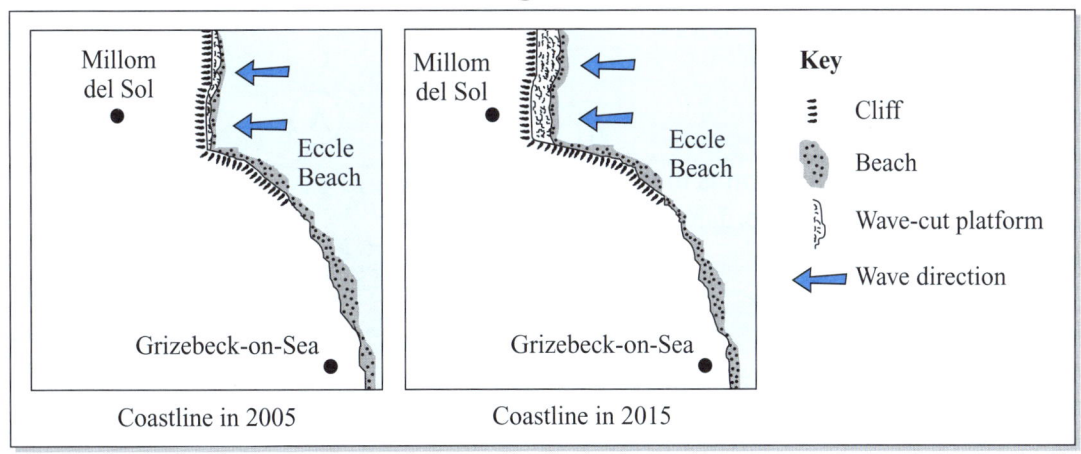

Figure 1

Coastline in 2005 | Coastline in 2015

Key:
- Cliff
- Beach
- Wave-cut platform
- Wave direction

a) Describe how the coastline shown in **Figure 1** changed between 2005 and 2015.

....
....
[2]

b) Name and describe **two** processes of erosion that could have caused the coastal change shown in **Figure 1**.

1:..
....
....

2:..
....
....
[4]

c) Explain how salt weathering can cause cliffs to break up.

....
....
....
....
[4]

d) Name a process of weathering, other than salt weathering, that could affect the cliffs in **Figure 1**.

....
[1]

[Total 11 marks]

Topic 4 — The UK's Evolving Physical Landscape

Coastal Landforms

1 Study **Figure 1**, a photograph showing coastal landforms.

Figure 1

a) Name the type of landform labelled A in **Figure 1**.

....
[1]

b) Identify whether this landform is most likely to be found on a concordant or discordant coastline.

....
[1]

c) Explain how the landforms shown in **Figure 1** are formed.

....
....
....
....
[3]
[Total 5 marks]

2 Study **Figure 2**, which shows **one** step in the formation of a wave-cut platform.

Figure 2

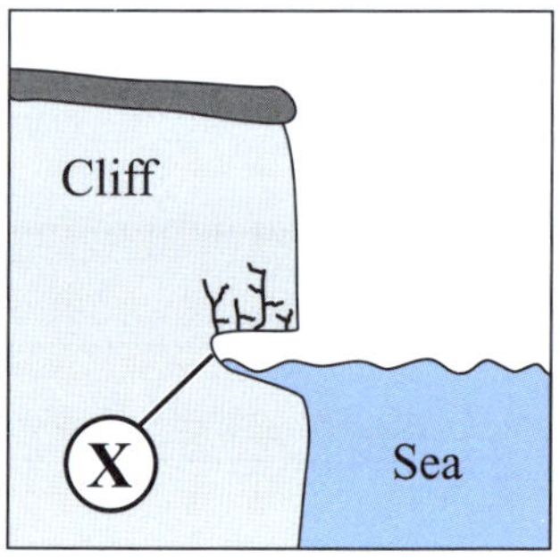

a) Name the feature indicated by label X in **Figure 2**.

....
[1]

b) Using **Figure 2**, explain how wave-cut platforms are formed.

....
....
....
....
[3]

c) Explain **two** ways in which climate can influence the rate of cliff retreat.

....
....
....
....
....
[4]
[Total 8 marks]

Topic 4 — The UK's Evolving Physical Landscape

Coastal Landforms

3 Study **Figure 3**, a photograph of a coastal area.

Figure 3

a) Name the type of landform labelled A in **Figure 3** and explain how it was formed.

Landform: ....
[1]

....
....
....
....
....
[2]

b) Use evidence from **Figure 3** to suggest what this coastal area may look like in the future. Explain your answer.

....
....
....
....
....
[4]

[Total 7 marks]

4 Study **Figure 4**, a graph showing how the width of a beach varied along its length in the years 2010 and 2015.

a) Using **Figure 4**, describe the width of the beach in 2010 compared with the width in 2015.

Figure 4

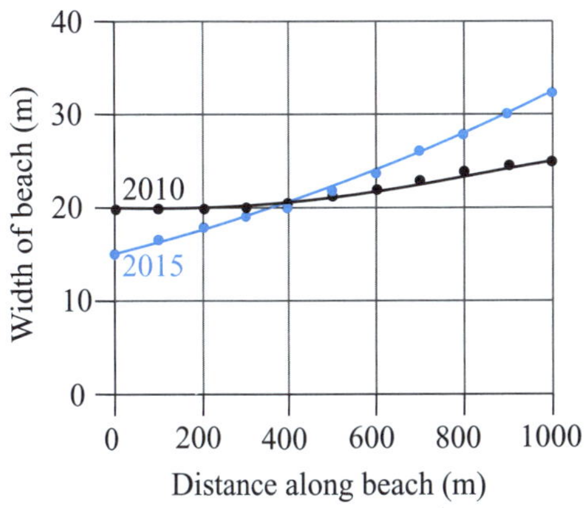

....
....
....
....
....
....
[3]

b) Name the type of wave acting on the stretch of coast shown in **Figure 4**.

....
[1]

Coastal Landforms

c) Give **two** characteristics of this type of wave.

1: ....

2: ....

[2]

d) Using a labelled diagram, explain the process of sediment transport that caused these changes in beach width.

[4]

[Total 10 marks]

5 Study **Figure 5**, an Ordnance Survey® map of a coastal area in Devon.

Figure 5

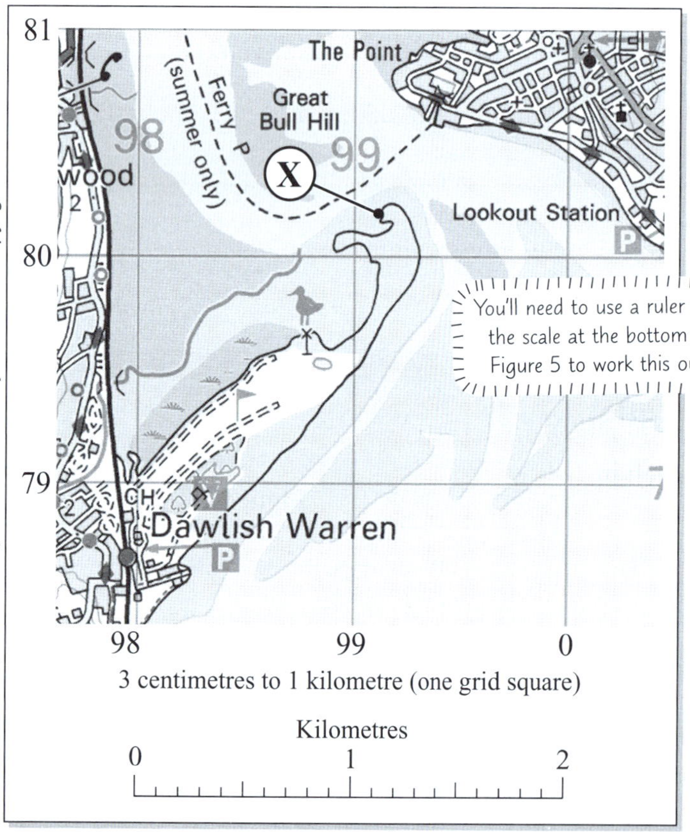

3 centimetres to 1 kilometre (one grid square)

a) The end of the spit is marked X on **Figure 5**. Give the six figure grid reference for the end of the spit.

....

[1]

b) What is the distance between the end of the spit and Dawlish Warren station at 979786?

You'll need to use a ruler and the scale at the bottom of Figure 5 to work this out.

.... km

[1]

c) Explain how the spit shown in **Figure 5** was formed.

....

....

....

....

....

[2]

d) Suggest what could happen to the spit in **Figure 5** if it continued to grow.

....

....

....

[2]

[Total 6 marks]

Human Activity at the Coast

1   Study **Figure 1**, a map of a coastal area.

Figure 1

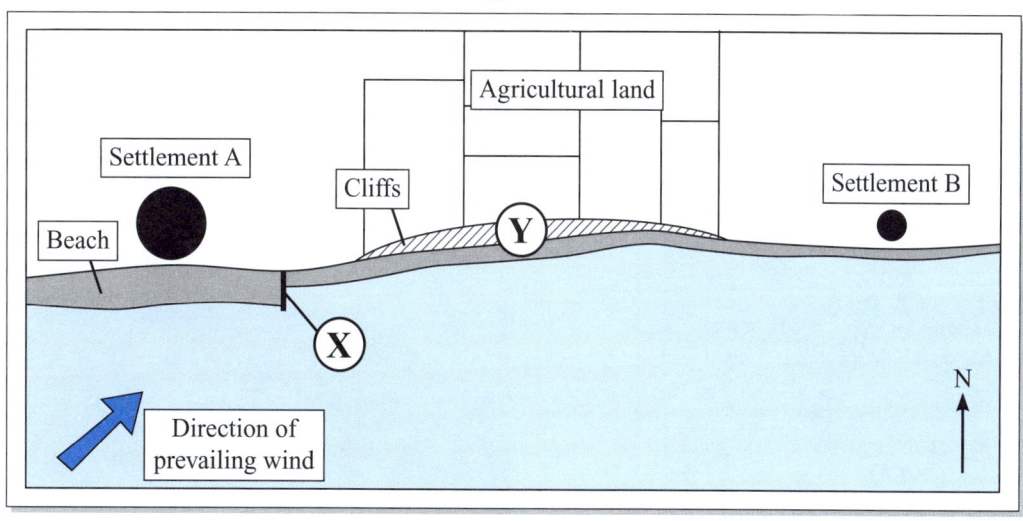

a)   In which direction is longshore drift occurring along the section of coast shown in **Figure 1**?

    A   North ◯

    B   South ◯

    C   East ◯

    D   West ◯

[1]

b)   Which of the following is likely to be an indirect effect of constructing the groyne at the point labelled X on **Figure 1**?

    A   The land at Settlement B is better protected.   ◯

    B   More sediment is transported along the coast.   ◯

    C   The beach in front of Settlement A will be narrower.   ◯

    D   Erosion at Settlement B is increased.   ◯

[1]

c)   Explain **one** way that using the land for agriculture, as shown in **Figure 1**, might affect the erosion of the cliffs at Y.

....

....

....

[2]

d)   Describe how the development of industry can affect coastal landscapes.

....

....

....

[2]

[Total 6 marks]

Topic 4 — The UK's Evolving Physical Landscape

Human Activity at the Coast

2   Study **Figures 2** and **3**. **Figure 2** shows a map of the Holderness coastline in the east of England. **Figure 3** shows a photograph of a cliff at Aldbrough.

Figure 2

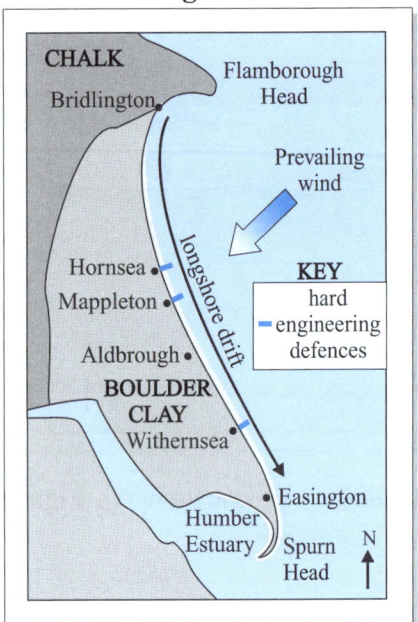

Figure 3

a) Using **Figure 2**, identify **two** ways the location of the coastline may be leading to high rates of erosion.

1:..

2:..
[2]

b) Explain how the location of the hard engineering defences might be changing the shape of the coastline.

....

....

....
[2]

c) Using **Figures 2** and **3**, suggest how the interaction of physical and human processes is influencing erosion at Aldbrough.

....

....

....

....

....
[4]
[Total 8 marks]

Coastal Flooding

1 Study **Figure 1**, which shows the frequencies of storms and floods between 2006 and 2015 in a coastal area of the UK.

Figure 1

Year	2006	2007	2008	2009	2010	2011	2012	2013	2014	2015
Number of storms	0	1	3	3	4	3	5	5	6	7
Number of floods	0	0	1	2	3	2	4	4	5	5

a) Calculate the mean number of floods per year.

....

....
[1]

b) Identify **one** way that the data could be presented to show the link between the number of storms and the number of floods.

....
[1]

c) Explain how storms can increase the frequency of coastal flooding.

....

....

....

....

....
[4]

d) Suggest **one** threat to people from increased frequency of coastal flooding.

....

....

....
[2]

e) Describe **one** way that coastal flooding has a negative impact on the environment.

....

....

....
[2]

[Total 10 marks]

Topic 4 — The UK's Evolving Physical Landscape

Coastal Management

1   Study **Figure 1**, a news article about coastal defences in Cliffall, a UK coastal town.

Figure 1

HOPE FOR CLIFFALL'S COASTLINE
Work is due to start next week on new defences for the Cliffall coastline. The town has been suffering from the effects of coastal erosion over the last few years but it's hoped the new defences will prevent further problems. The scheme will use a combination of defences, including groynes, slope stabilisation and beach replenishment. The work will be completed gradually over the next four years, with the groynes the top priority.

a) Which **one** of the coastal management strategies below is a hard engineering strategy?

   A   Beach replenishment   ○
   B   Slope stabilisation   ○
   C   Groynes   ○
   D   Strategic realignment   ○

   [1]

b) Explain how **one** soft engineering strategy mentioned in **Figure 1** can protect the coastline.

   ....
   ....
   ....
   [2]

c) Give **one** disadvantage of the soft engineering strategy identified in part b).

   ....
   [1]

d) Suggest why the coastal management strategy for Cliffall does not include strategic realignment.

   ....
   ....
   [2]

e) Explain how Integrated Coastal Zone Management can offer a sustainable approach to protecting the coastline.

   ....
   ....
   ....
   ....
   [3]

   [Total 9 marks]

River Processes and Landscapes

1 Study **Figure 1**, which shows the long profile of a river.

a) Which part of the river is labelled A in **Figure 1**?

   A   Mouth ○
   B   Source ○
   C   Lower course ○
   D   Channel ○

   [1]

   Figure 1 (long profile graph: Height above sea level (m) 0–500 vs Distance along river (km) 0–300, with points A near source, B partway down, C near mouth)

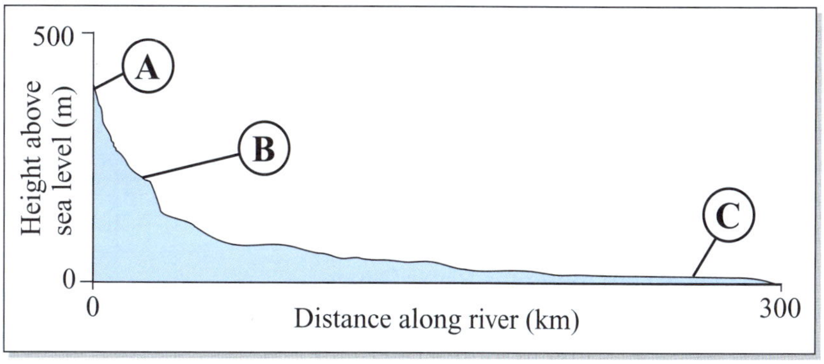

b) Which of the following statements best describes how sediment size and shape change over a river's course?

   A   Sediment becomes smaller and more well-rounded along a river's course. ○
   B   Sediment gets larger and more angular towards the mouth of a river. ○
   C   Sediment remains roughly the same size and shape along the course of a river. ○
   D   The size of sediment changes along the course of a river, but sediment shape remains the same. ○

   [1]

c) Explain how river discharge changes along the course of a river.

   ....
   ....
   ....
   [2]

d) Compare the long and cross profiles of the upper course of a river valley with the lower course.

   ....
   ....
   ....
   ....
   [3]

e) Explain how freeze-thaw weathering could shape a river valley in the upper course.

   ....
   ....
   ....
   ....
   [4]

   [Total 11 marks]

Topic 4 — The UK's Evolving Physical Landscape

River Processes and Landscapes

2   Study **Figure 2**, which shows how river velocity and particle size vary along the River Dance.

a) Small gravel particles are transported by velocities above 0.1 m per second.
At what distance along the River Dance does the transportation of gravel start?

....
[1]

b) At 80 km along the River Dance, pebbles are being transported.
Give the velocity of the river at this point.

....
[1]

c) Identify the most likely process by which pebbles are transported in the River Dance.

....
[1]

Figure 2

d) Using **Figure 2**, suggest why deposition is the dominant process between 20 and 30 km.

....
....
....
[2]

e) Explain why velocity increases along the river's course.

....
....
....
[2]

f) Explain **two** processes of erosion that are likely to be deepening the river channel in the upper course of the River Dance.

1:..
....
....

2:..
....
....
[4]

[Total 11 marks]

Topic 4 — The UK's Evolving Physical Landscape

River Landforms

1 Study **Figure 1**, which is an Ordnance Survey® map showing part of Snowdonia, Wales.

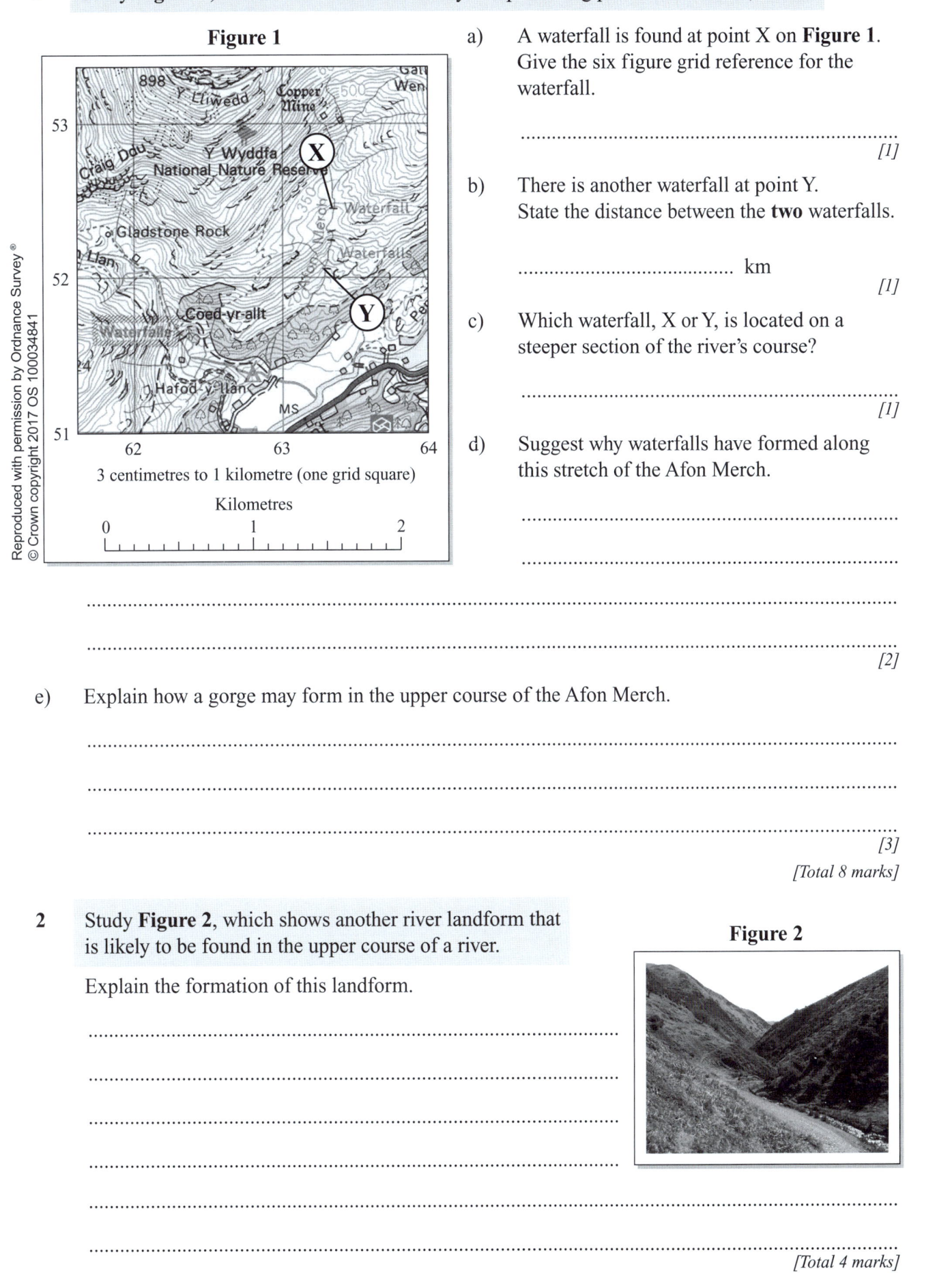

Figure 1

a) A waterfall is found at point X on **Figure 1**. Give the six figure grid reference for the waterfall.

....
[1]

b) There is another waterfall at point Y. State the distance between the **two** waterfalls.

.... km
[1]

c) Which waterfall, X or Y, is located on a steeper section of the river's course?

....
[1]

d) Suggest why waterfalls have formed along this stretch of the Afon Merch.

....
....
....
....
[2]

e) Explain how a gorge may form in the upper course of the Afon Merch.

....
....
....
[3]

[Total 8 marks]

2 Study **Figure 2**, which shows another river landform that is likely to be found in the upper course of a river.

Explain the formation of this landform.

Figure 2

....
....
....
....
....
[Total 4 marks]

Topic 4 — The UK's Evolving Physical Landscape

River Landforms

3   Study **Figure 3**, which is a labelled photograph of a meander.

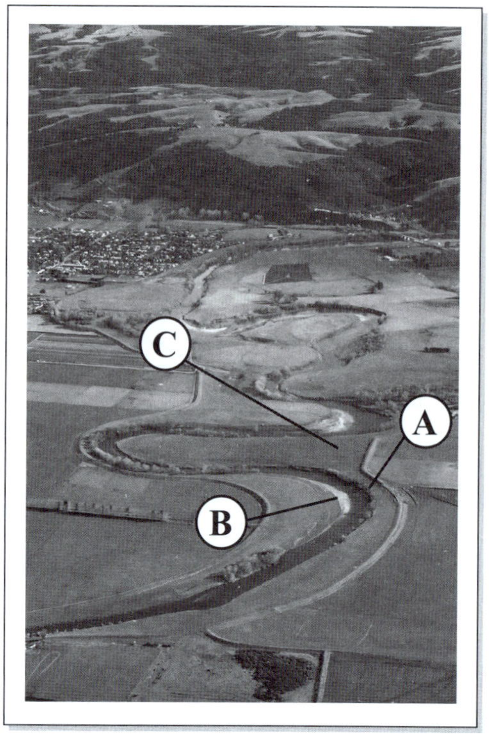

a) Name a feature likely to be found at the part of the river labelled A in **Figure 3** and explain its formation.

    ....
    ....
    ....
    ....
    ....
    ....
    [3]

Figure 3

b) Name a feature likely to be found at the part of the river labelled B in **Figure 3** and explain its formation.

    ....
    ....
    ....
    ....
    ....
    ....
    [3]

c) Name the feature labelled C in **Figure 3**.

    ....
    [1]

d) Using a labelled diagram, explain how an ox-bow lake could form on the river shown in **Figure 3**.

[4]

[Total 11 marks]

Topic 4 — The UK's Evolving Physical Landscape

River Landforms

4 Study **Figure 4**, a cross profile of a river.

a) Identify the feature labelled Y on **Figure 4**.

A   Levee   ◯
B   Estuary   ◯
C   Flood plain   ◯
D   Gorge   ◯

[1]

Figure 4

b) Explain how the landform labelled Y in **Figure 4** is formed.

....
....
....
....
[3]

c) Explain how the landform labelled Z in **Figure 4** builds up over time.

....
....
....
[2]
[Total 6 marks]

5 **Figure 5** shows a photograph of a delta in Inversanda Bay, Scotland.

Figure 5

Explain the processes involved in the formation of the landform shown in **Figure 5**.

....
....
....
....
....
....
....
....
....
[Total 4 marks]

Topic 4 — The UK's Evolving Physical Landscape

River Landscapes and Sediment Load

1   River landscapes and sediment load are affected by a variety of physical processes.

a)   Which of the following best describes the influence of geology on sediment load?

   A   Hard rock erodes quickly leading to a high sediment load.   ○
   B   Hard rock erodes slowly leading to a low sediment load.   ○
   C   Soft rock erodes quickly leading to a low sediment load.   ○
   D   Soft rock erodes slowly leading to a high sediment load.   ○

   [1]

b)   Explain **two** ways in which climate influences sediment load.

   1: ....
   ....
   ....
   2: ....
   ....
   ....
   [4]

c)   Describe the process of soil creep.

   ....
   ....
   ....
   [2]

d)   Study **Figure 1**, a photo of an upland landscape in Scotland. Explain the effect of climate on the landscape shown.

   Figure 1

   ....
   ....
   ....
   ....
   ....
   [2]

   [Total 9 marks]

Topic 4 — The UK's Evolving Physical Landscape

River Discharge and Flooding

1   Study **Figure 1**, which shows storm hydrographs for two rivers.

Figure 1

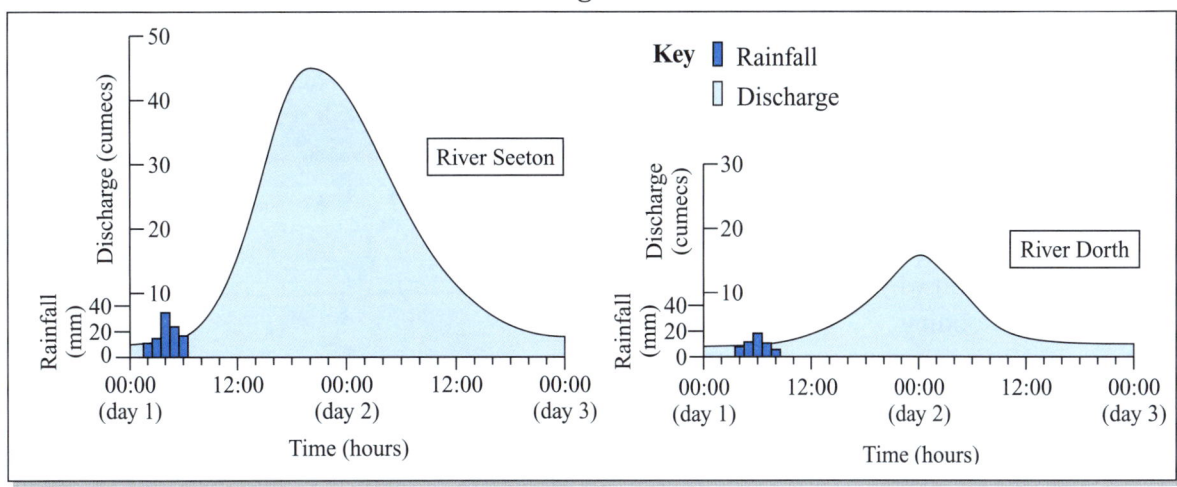

a)   At what time was the River Seeton at peak discharge?

....
[1]

b)   Peak rainfall around the River Dorth was at 06:00 on day 1. What was the lag time?

....
[1]

c)   Explain which river is more likely to flood.

....

....

....
[2]

d)   The land around the River Seeton has been paved and built on. Suggest how land use in the catchment of the River Seeton might affect the shape of the hydrograph in **Figure 1**.

....

....

....
[2]

e)   Explain how the shape of a drainage basin can affect the shape of a storm hydrograph.

....

....

....
[2]

[Total 8 marks]

River Discharge and Flooding

2   Study **Figure 2**, a map of the Eden basin in the north west of England. There was severe flooding in the Eden basin in 2015, partly due to the antecedent conditions experienced.

a) What is meant by the term 'antecedent conditions'?

    ....
    ....
    [1]

Figure 2

Key:
- Softer rocks
- Harder rocks
- Upland areas
- ---- Watershed
- ● Urban areas

(Carlisle, North Pennines, Lake District)

b) Give **one** reason why soil type affects the risk of flooding.

    ....
    ....
    ....
    [1]

c) Using evidence from **Figure 2**, explain why flooding is likely in the city of Carlisle.

    ....
    ....
    ....
    ....
    ....
    [4]

d) Explain **two** reasons why flood risk is increasing in the UK.

    1: ....
    ....
    ....

    2: ....
    ....
    ....
    [4]

e) State **two** threats to people from more frequent flooding.

    1: ....
    2: ....
    [2]

    [Total 12 marks]

Topic 4 — The UK's Evolving Physical Landscape

River Management

1 Study **Figure 1**, which shows some of the engineering strategies used to combat flooding along the River Joiner.

Figure 1

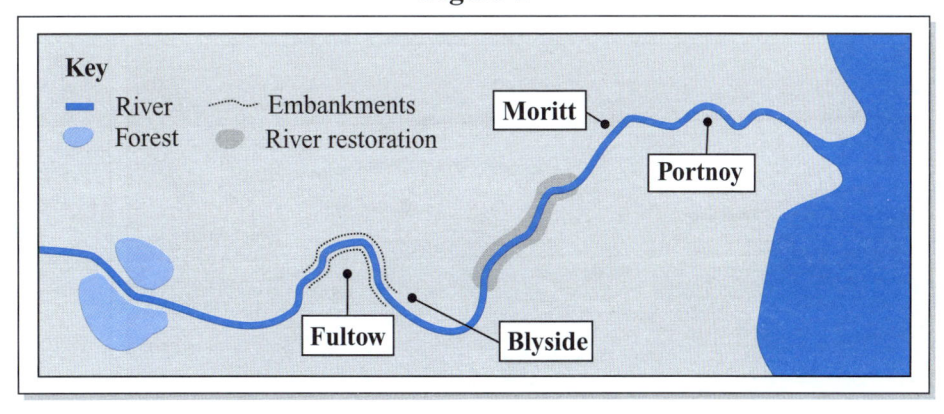

Key
— River   ····· Embankments
● Forest   ▓ River restoration

(Locations shown: Moritt, Portnoy, Fultow, Blyside)

a) Using **Figure 1**, identify **one** hard engineering strategy being used to manage flooding on the River Joiner.

....
[1]

b) Explain how river restoration, as shown in **Figure 1**, may reduce the risk of flooding in Moritt.

....
....
....
[2]

c) Give **one** advantage of using embankments instead of flood walls to protect the town of Fultow.

....
[1]

d) Explain how the embankments used at Fultow could cause problems at Blyside.

....
....
....
[2]

e) Explain why there may be objections to using flood plain retention to manage flood risk at Portnoy.

....
....
....
[2]

[Total 8 marks]

Topic 4 — The UK's Evolving Physical Landscape

Investigating a UK Geographical Issue

1 Study **Figure 1**, which shows a stretch of coastline in the south west of the UK that's retreating. The beach width varies along the coastline and the beaches are backed by cliffs.

Figure 1

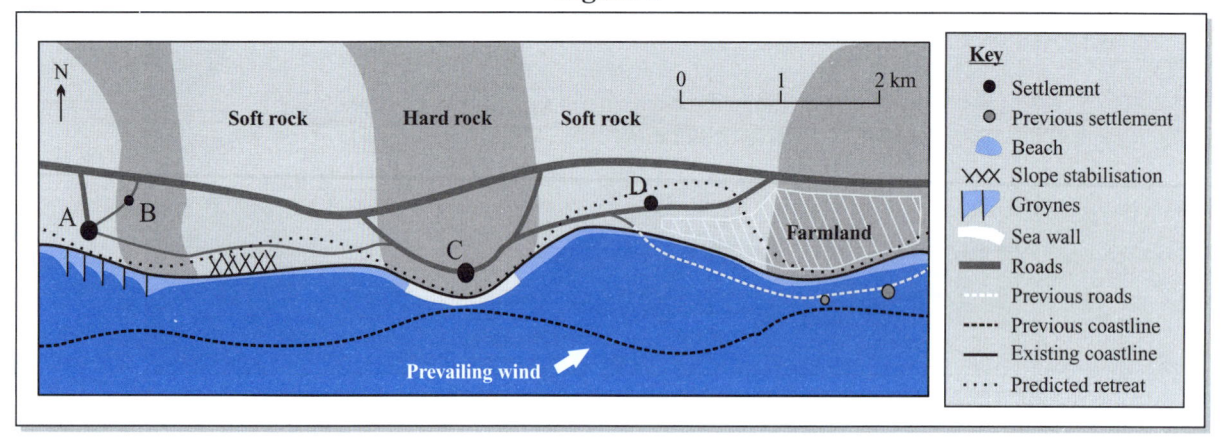

a) Using **Figure 1** and your own knowledge, evaluate the choice of coastal management strategies for the long-term sustainable management of the stretch of coastline shown.

[8]

b) Assess the extent to which human and physical processes are causing change on the stretch of coastline shown in **Figure 1**.

[8 + 4 SPaG]
[Total 20 marks]

2 Study **Figure 2**, a map of the UK showing the location of major rivers and areas of possible flood risk, and **Figure 3**, showing population density in the UK.

Figure 2

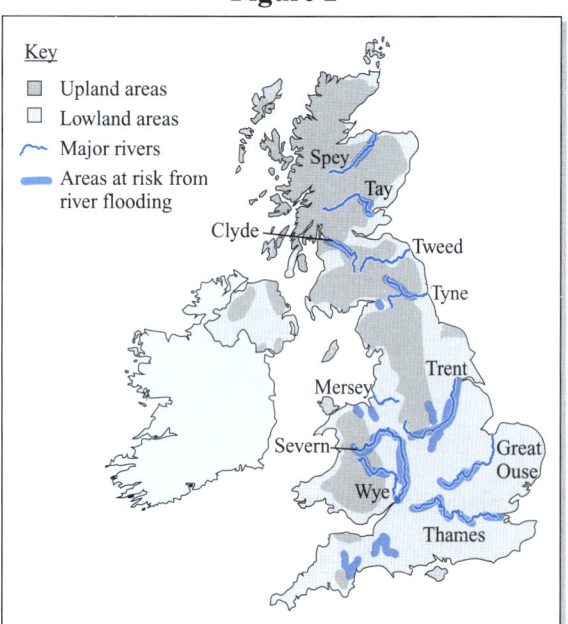

Figure 3

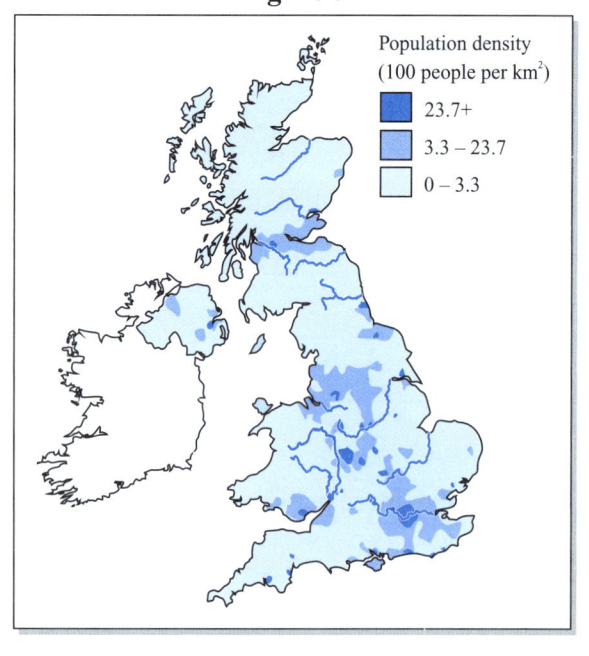

Assess the extent to which human and physical factors might be affecting the number of people at risk from river flooding in the UK.

[8 + 4 SPaG]
[Total 12 marks]

Topic 4 — The UK's Evolving Physical Landscape

Topic 5 — The UK's Evolving Human Landscape

UK Human Landscape

1   Study **Figure 1**, a map showing the population density of the UK.

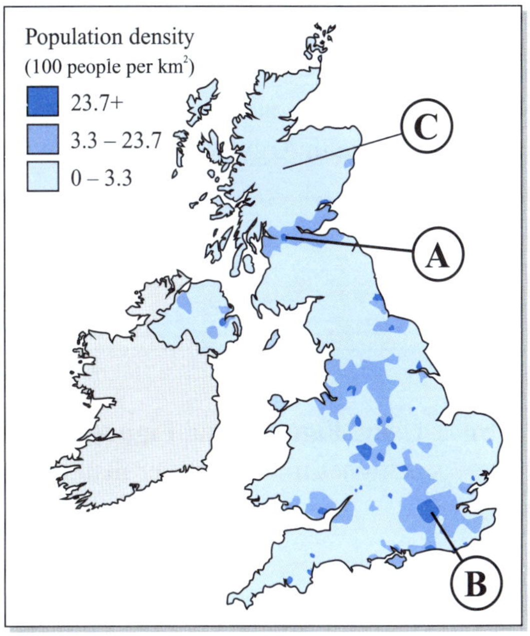

a) Describe the pattern of population density in the UK.

....
....
....
....
[2]

Figure 1

Population density (100 people per km²)
- 23.7+
- 3.3 – 23.7
- 0 – 3.3

b) Name the cities labelled A and B in **Figure 1**.

A: ....

B: ....
[2]

c) State **one** reason why the area labelled C on **Figure 1** has a low population density.

....
[1]

d) Which **one** of the following statements about the distribution of areas with high concentrations of economic activity in the UK is true?

   A   They are usually in rural areas.   ○
   B   Most are in northern Scotland.   ○
   C   There are none in Wales.   ○
   D   There are lots in south-east England.   ○
[1]

e) **Figure 2** is a map of the UK showing the distribution of people over the age of 65. Explain the relationship between population density and the distribution of people over 65 in the UK.

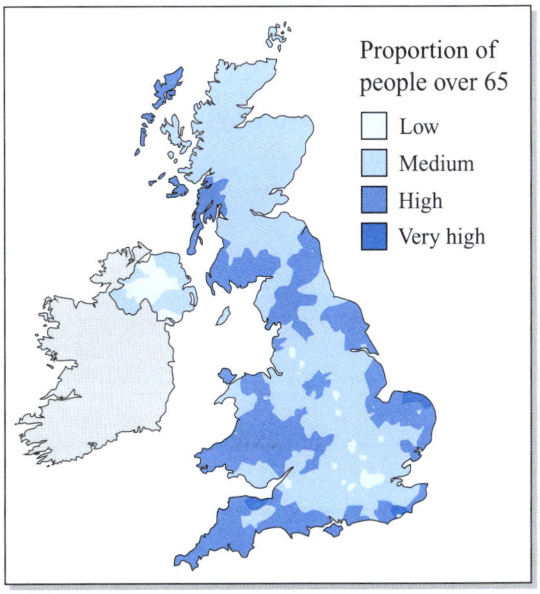

....
....
....
....
....
....
....
....
[4]

[Total 10 marks]

Figure 2

Proportion of people over 65
- Low
- Medium
- High
- Very high

UK Human Landscape

2 Study **Figure 3**, which shows population and job density statistics for Manchester (urban) and Argyll and Bute (rural), and **Figure 4**, which shows the location of these areas and major transport links in the UK.

a) State **one** possible economic reason for the population change in Argyll and Bute shown in **Figure 3**.

....

....

....
[1]

Figure 3

	Manchester	Argyll and Bute
Percentage change in population (2001-2011)	+28.08	-3.44
Job density* (2015)	1.07	0.88

*ratio of total jobs to working age population

b) Using **Figure 2** and **Figure 3**, explain why job density is higher in Manchester than in Argyll and Bute.

....

....

....

....

....
[2]

c) Explain how a regional development fund could be used to reduce the regional variation between Argyll and Bute and Manchester.

....

....

....

....

....
[2]

Figure 4

Key: motorways, railways

d) Describe **two** ways that the UK government is trying to reduce regional inequalities.

1:..

....

....

2:..

....

....
[4]

[Total 9 marks]

Topic 5 — The UK's Evolving Human Landscape

Migration

1 Study **Figure 1**, a table showing net international migration into the UK between 2001 and 2015.

a) Using **Figure 1**, calculate the range of the net international migration values.

....
[1]

Figure 1

	Net international migration
2001	153 200
2002	190 900
2003	194 200
2004	209 900
2005	336 000
2006	254 800
2007	304 900
2008	284 100
2009	220 100
2010	255 600
2011	270 500
2012	165 500
2013	188 500
2014	264 900
2015	341 400

b) Explain how international migration has altered the age structure of the UK.

....

....

....

....

....

....

....

....
[4]

c) State **two** trends in national migration in the UK.

1:...

2:...
[2]

[Total 7 marks]

2 The ethnic diversity of the UK has changed over the last 60 years.

Explain how the government's immigration policy has changed the UK's diversity.

....

....

....

....

....

....

[Total 4 marks]

Topic 5 — The UK's Evolving Human Landscape

The UK Economy

1 Study **Figure 1**, photographs of central Newcastle Upon Tyne in 1929 and 2015.

Figure 1

a) Using **Figure 1** and your own knowledge, describe how the economy of Newcastle may have changed between 1929 and 2015.

....

....

....
[2]

b) Give **one** possible reason for the changes shown in **Figure 1**.

....

....
[1]
[Total 3 marks]

2 Study **Figure 2**, a graph showing change in the percentage of people employed in different sectors in the UK between 2001 and 2014.

Figure 2

a) Using **Figure 2**, state the percentage by which the number of people employed in education increased.

....
[1]

b) Give **one** reason why professional and technical employment has increased.

....

....

....

....
[1]
[Total 2 marks]

Topic 5 — The UK's Evolving Human Landscape

UK Links with the Wider World

1 Study **Figure 1**, a table showing the number of new foreign direct investments (FDI) in the UK each year from 2011 to 2016.

Figure 1

Year	2011/12	2012/13	2013/14	2014/15	2015/16
Number of new FDI	752	777	820	1058	1130

a) Using **Figure 1**, calculate the percentage increase in new investments between 2014/15 and 2015/16.

....

....
[2]

b) Explain how globalisation has increased FDI in the UK.

....

....

....

....

....
[4]

c) Name **one** factor, other than globalisation, that has contributed to the increase in FDI in the UK.

....
[1]
[Total 7 marks]

2 There are lots of transnational corporations (TNCs) in the UK.

a) State **one** positive effect that TNCs have had on the UK economy.

....

....
[1]

b) Suggest **one** possible negative effect of over-reliance on TNCs in the UK.

....

....

....
[2]
[Total 3 marks]

Topic 5 — The UK's Evolving Human Landscape

Dynamic UK Cities

1 Study **Figure 1**, a map of central Newcastle, a regenerated city centre.

a) Give **two** pieces of evidence from **Figure 1** that indicate that the area shown is the CBD.

1:..
....
....

2:..
....
....
[2]

Figure 1

(Map of central Newcastle showing: To Newcastle International Airport, Financial services, Law firms, New arts and music centre. Key: motorway, A-road, B-road, other road, railway, railway station, U university, River Tyne. Scale 0 m – 500 m. Contains OS data © Crown copyright and database right (2017))

b) Regeneration of a city often involves 'rebranding'. What is meant by this term?

....
....
[1]

c) Give **two** possible sources of economic growth in central Newcastle.

1:..
2:..
[2]

d) For a UK city you have studied, explain why some areas of the city have declined.

....
....
....
....
....
[4]

e) For a named city in the UK, explain **two** strategies that have been used to make the city more sustainable.

1:..
....
2:..
....
[4]

[Total 13 marks]

Topic 5 — The UK's Evolving Human Landscape

Dynamic UK Cities

2 Study **Figure 2**, which shows an area of Byrnshire in 1950 and 2016.

a) State **two** ways that cities and the rural areas around them depend on each other.

1: ....

....

....

2: ....

....

....

....
[2]

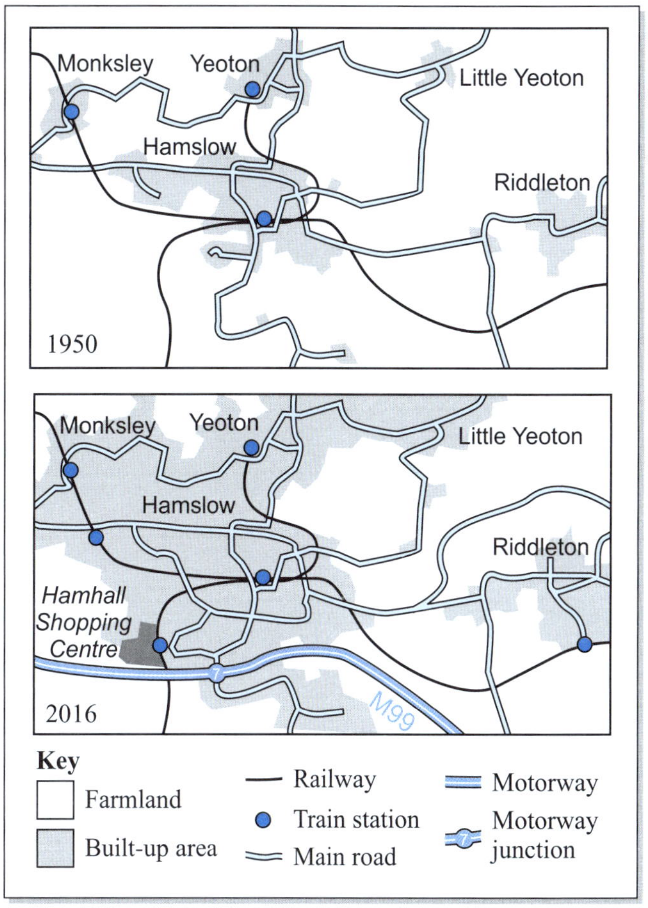

b) Using **Figure 2**, describe **one** environmental cost of the changes to the rural area around Hamslow between 1950 and 2016.

....

....

....

....

....
[2]

Figure 2

c) Suggest **one** social challenge that Riddleton might face due to its links with the city of Hamslow.

....

....

....
[2]

[Total 6 marks]

3 Study **Figure 3**, a graph showing the migration of males into and out of London in 2013 across a range of age groups.

a) Using **Figure 3**, which age group experienced a net increase in population due to migration?

    A   0-10 years   ◯

    B   11-20 years   ◯

    C   21-30 years   ◯

    D   31-40 years   ◯

[1]

Figure 3

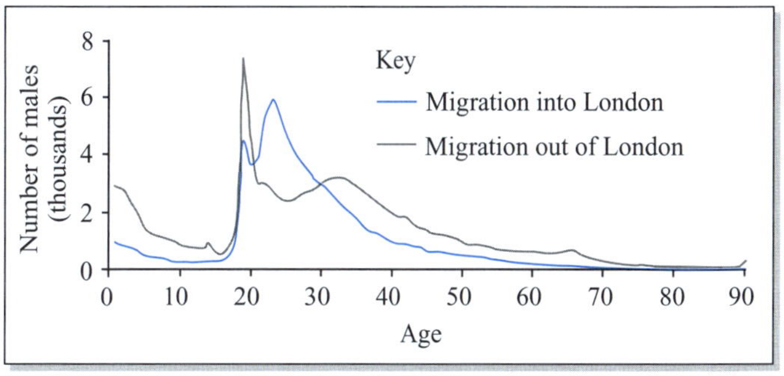

Topic 5 — The UK's Evolving Human Landscape

Dynamic UK Cities

b) Explain the patterns of migration for a named UK city.

....

....

....

....

....
[4]

c) For a UK city that you have studied, describe **two** ways in which migration into the city has affected its character.

1: ....

....

....

2: ....

....

....
[4]

[Total 9 marks]

Investigating a UK Geographical Issue

4 Analyse **Figure 4**, which shows the Index of Multiple Deprivation (IMD) ranking of different areas in the West Midlands. The IMD ranks every neighbourhood in England, with the most deprived having a rank of 1. The table also shows where these neighbourhoods rank in England for employment, health and housing and services deprivation.

Figure 4

Location	IMD Rank	Employment deprivation Rank	Health deprivation Rank	Housing and services deprivation Rank
Aston (inner city)	668	324	6747	235
Kings Heath (suburb)	7392	11 124	8712	16 684
Hampton-in-Arden (commuter village)	30 336	30 571	29 492	11 417
Diddlebury (rural village)	12 311	24 319	23 657	177

Assess the reasons for variation in IMD in cities and their surrounding areas.

[8 + 4 SPaG]

[Total 12 marks]

Topic 5 — The UK's Evolving Human Landscape

Topic 6 — Geographical Investigations

Fieldwork in a Physical Environment

1   You have carried out fieldwork in **either** a coastal **or** river environment.

You might not have completed your fieldwork yet — don't start this section until your enquiry is finished.

Name your coastal/river environment fieldwork location.

....

a) Explain how your fieldwork enquiry improved your understanding of an area of geography.

....

....

....

....

[3]

b) Describe **one** of the quantitative data collection techniques that you used.

....

....

....

[2]

c) Explain how **one** of your primary data collection techniques was appropriate to the task.

....

....

....

....

[3]

d) Describe **two** strengths of **one** of the data presentation techniques that you used.

Data presentation technique:..

1:...

....

....

2:...

....

....

[4]

Fieldwork in a Physical Environment

e) Explain **one** way that the use of maps was helpful in your investigation.

   ....
   ....
   ....
   [2]

f) Explain why the statistical techniques you used to analyse your data were appropriate.

   ....
   ....
   ....
   ....
   ....
   ....
   [4]

g) Using an annotated diagram, explain **either**
   - the effectiveness of **one** coastal management measure you studied, **or**
   - **one** factor influencing the flood risk at the river you studied.

   [4]

h) Assess the extent to which your results allowed you to reach a valid conclusion to your original question.

   [8]
   [Total 30 marks]

Investigating Coastal Change and Conflict

1   A student wanted to investigate how the cross-profile of a beach is affected by different coastal management strategies along the shore. **Figure 1** shows the method she used to find the cross-profile of the beach. She measured the profile at three points along the beach. The results are shown in **Figure 2**.

If you studied rivers for your fieldwork enquiry you don't need to answer these questions — there are questions about rivers on the next page.

Figure 1

Angle between ranging poles, measured with a clinometer
Ranging poles placed at 5m intervals
5m
Beach
Sea
Measurements started at low tide mark and repeated to top of beach

Figure 2

Height (m) vs Distance from low water mark (m), showing three curves labelled A, B, and C.

a)   Describe **two** possible sources of inaccuracy in the method used.

   1:..

   ....

   2:..

   ....
   [2]

b)   Suggest how the student might have chosen the points along the beach at which to measure the cross-profiles.

   ....

   ....
   [2]

c)   Suggest **one** way in which the student could add to **Figure 2** so that the data is presented more effectively.

   ....

   ....
   [2]

d)   Suggest **one** way in which the reliability of the data could be improved.

   ....

   ....
   [2]

   [Total 8 marks]

Topic 6 — Geographical Investigations

Investigating River Processes and Pressures

1   As part of a fieldwork enquiry into factors influencing flood risk, a student collected data on river velocity. He placed a float in the river and recorded the time taken for the float to travel 10 metres downstream. The results are shown in **Figure 1**.

a) State **one** appropriate item that could be used as the float.
Give **one** reason for your answer.

Item: ....

Reason: ....

....

....
[1]

Figure 1

Sample	Time (s)
1	315
2	255
3	278
4	310
5	947
6	302
7	279
8	297

b) Identify the sample in the data that is an anomaly.

....
[1]

c) Suggest **one** possible reason for the anomaly.

....

....

....
[2]

d) The student also measured the depth of the river with a metre ruler.
Describe **one** possible source of inaccuracy in this method.

....

....

....
[2]

e) Describe **one** source of qualitative data that the student could collect as part of his investigation into factors affecting flood risk.

....

....

....
[2]

[Total 8 marks]

Topic 6 — Geographical Investigations

Fieldwork in a Human Environment

1   You have carried out fieldwork investigating variations in the quality of life in **either** an urban **or** a rural area.

   Name your urban/rural environment fieldwork location.

   ....

a) Explain why you used **one** of the primary data collection techniques involved in your enquiry.

   Primary data collection technique: ....

   Explanation: ....

   ....

   ....
   [2]

b) Explain which sampling technique (e.g. random, stratified or systematic) was best suited to your investigation.

   ....

   ....

   ....
   [2]

c) State **two** ways in which you managed the risks associated with your fieldwork.

   1: ....

   ....

   2: ....

   ....
   [2]

d) You used census data in your investigation. Explain how this data source was useful.

   ....

   ....

   ....
   [2]

Topic 6 — Geographical Investigations

Fieldwork in a Human Environment

e) Other than the data you collected, suggest **one** source of data that would have helped you to answer your original question. Give a reason for your answer.

....

....

....
[2]

f) Explain how you adapted your data presentation techniques to show your results effectively.

....

....

....
[2]

g) Explain **one** limitation of your data presentation methods.

....

....

....
[2]

h) Explain how collecting data on environmental quality allowed you to reach conclusions about why quality of life varies within the area you studied.

....

....

....

....

....

....
[4]

i) Evaluate the suitability of the sites you chose for data collection.
[8]

[Total 26 marks]

Investigating Dynamic Urban Areas

1   A group of students is investigating how and why the quality of life varies within the city of Suninsky. One of their data sources is the 2010 Index of Multiple Deprivation (IMD). The IMD for each ward in Suninsky is presented in **Figure 1**.

Only do this page if your enquiry was about urban areas — the next page covers rural areas.

Figure 1

a)   Give **one** primary data collection method that could be used to support this investigation.

....

....
[1]

b)   Explain how suitable it is for the students to use data from the 2010 Index of Multiple Deprivation in their investigation.

....

....

....

....

....

....

....
[4]

c)   Explain **one** limitation of using a choropleth map to show deprivation in **Figure 1**.

....

....

....
[2]

d)   The students decided to go to the three sites marked with dots on the map to collect primary data. Explain how suitable this choice of sites is for this investigation.

....

....

....

....
[2]

[Total 9 marks]

Topic 6 — Geographical Investigations

Investigating Changing Rural Areas

1   Some students investigated how quality of life varies in the rural area surrounding their school. They carried out environmental quality surveys at several sites by scoring various factors on a bipolar scale. The bipolar analysis table they used for data collection is shown in **Figure 1**.

Figure 1

Low quality	Environmental quality score							High quality
	-3	-2	-1	0	+1	+2	+3	
Very noisy								No noise pollution
Heavily littered								No litter
Obvious vandalism								No evidence of vandalism
Roads and pavements poorly maintained								Roads and pavements well maintained

a) Suggest **one** possible limitation of using this data collection method.

....

....

....
[2]

b) Suggest **one** way that the data from the environmental quality survey could be presented.

....

....

....
[2]

c) State **one** other primary data collection method that could be used in this investigation.

....
[1]

d) Describe **one** way that secondary data could be used to support the investigation.

....

....

....
[2]

[Total 7 marks]

Topic 6 — Geographical Investigations

Topic 7 — People and the Biosphere

Global Ecosystems

1 Study **Figure 1**, a map showing the distribution of some of the world's biomes.

Figure 1

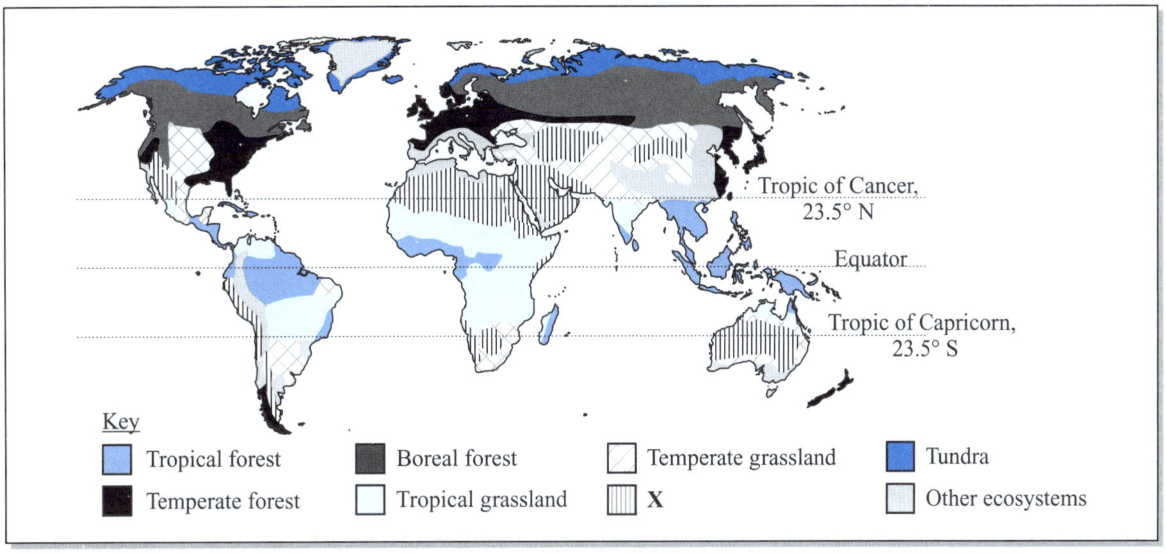

Key:
- Tropical forest
- Temperate forest
- Boreal forest
- Tropical grassland
- Temperate grassland
- X
- Tundra
- Other ecosystems

a) Define the term 'biome'.

....

....
[1]

b) Identify the biome labelled 'X' in **Figure 1**.

....
[1]

c) Using **Figure 1**, describe the global distribution of tropical forests.

....

....

....
[2]

d) Describe the climate in tundra environments.

....

....

....
[2]

[Total 6 marks]

2 Biomes are made up of biotic and abiotic components.

a) Name **one** biotic and **one** abiotic component found in biomes.

Biotic: ....

Abiotic: ....
[2]

Global Ecosystems

b) Describe **two** ways that biotic components interact with abiotic components in an ecosystem.

1:..

....

2:..

....
[4]

[Total 6 marks]

3   Study **Figure 2**, which shows climate data for a hot desert.

a) Using **Figure 2**, identify the average maximum temperature for December.

.... °C

[1]

Figure 2

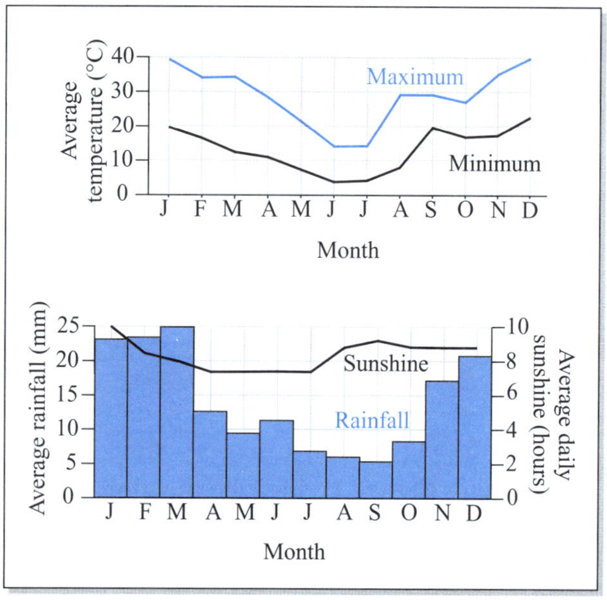

b) With reference to **Figure 2**, describe **two** characteristics of the hot desert climate.

Characteristic 1: ....

....

....

....

Characteristic 2: ....

....

....
[4]

c) Explain how **two** factors other than climate can influence the local distribution of biomes.

Factor 1:...

....

....

Factor 2:...

....

....
[4]

[Total 9 marks]

Global Ecosystems

4 Study **Figure 3**, a photograph of savannah grassland.

a) Using **Figure 3** and your own knowledge, describe the flora of grassland ecosystems.

....
....
....
....
....
[2]

Figure 3

b) Which statement best describes the characteristics of the vegetation of tundra ecosystems?

    A   The vegetation is evergreen because the climate is cold all year round. ◯

    B   The trees drop their leaves in the winter to cope with the colder weather. ◯

    C   The vegetation is dense because winters are long. ◯

    D   The vegetation is stunted because the growing season is very short. ◯

[1]

[Total 3 marks]

5 Study **Figure 4**, which shows temperature and rainfall data for an area of forest.

a) Which month has the highest average temperature?

....
[1]

b) Identify the type of forest biome that is likely to have developed in the climate shown in **Figure 4**.

....
[1]

c) Describe the vegetation found in this type of forest.

....
....
....
....
[2]

[Total 4 marks]

Figure 4

Month	Average temperature / °C	Average rainfall / mm
January	2	64
February	5	42
March	6	33
April	12	42
May	19	45
June	19	48
July	21	69
August	19	62
September	12	45
October	10	55
November	4	65
December	2	52

Topic 7 — People and the Biosphere

Humans and the Biosphere

1 The biosphere provides humans with lots of resources.

a) State **two** commercial resources that humans exploit the biosphere for.

1:...

2:...
[2]

b) Describe **two** ways that tropical forests provide goods and services for indigenous and local people.

1:...

....

....

2:...

....

....
[4]
[Total 6 marks]

2 Study **Figure 1**, a table showing forest cover in Terra Spoglio between 1970 and 2010.

Figure 1

Year	Area of forest cover remaining (million ha)
1970	5.42
1980	5.40
1990	4.89
2000	4.61
2010	4.04

a) Using **Figure 1**, calculate the percentage change in forest cover between 1970 and 2010.

....

....

....
[2]

b) The total area of Terra Spoglio is 19 million hectares. Calculate the percentage of Terra Spoglio that was covered by forest in 1990.

....
[1]

c) Describe how increasing demand for energy is causing deforestation of the biosphere.

....

....

....
[2]
[Total 5 marks]

Topic 7 — People and the Biosphere

Role of the Biosphere

1 The biosphere provides globally important services.

a) Which **one** of the following is a globally important service provided by the biosphere?

    A Reducing the impacts of volcanic eruptions. ○

    B Regulating the amount of solar radiation the Earth receives. ○

    C Regulating the water cycle. ○

    D Modifying geology in order to reduce erosion. ○

[1]

b) Explain **two** ways that the biosphere regulates the nutrient content of the soil.

1:..

....

....

2:..

....

....

[4]

c) Explain **one** way that the biosphere functions to prevent droughts or floods in some areas.

....

....

....

[2]

d) Explain how changes to the biosphere may change the composition of the atmosphere.

....

....

....

....

....

[3]

[Total 10 marks]

Topic 7 — People and the Biosphere

Demand for Resources

1 Study **Figure 1**, a graph showing real and projected changes in global population from 1950 to 2050.

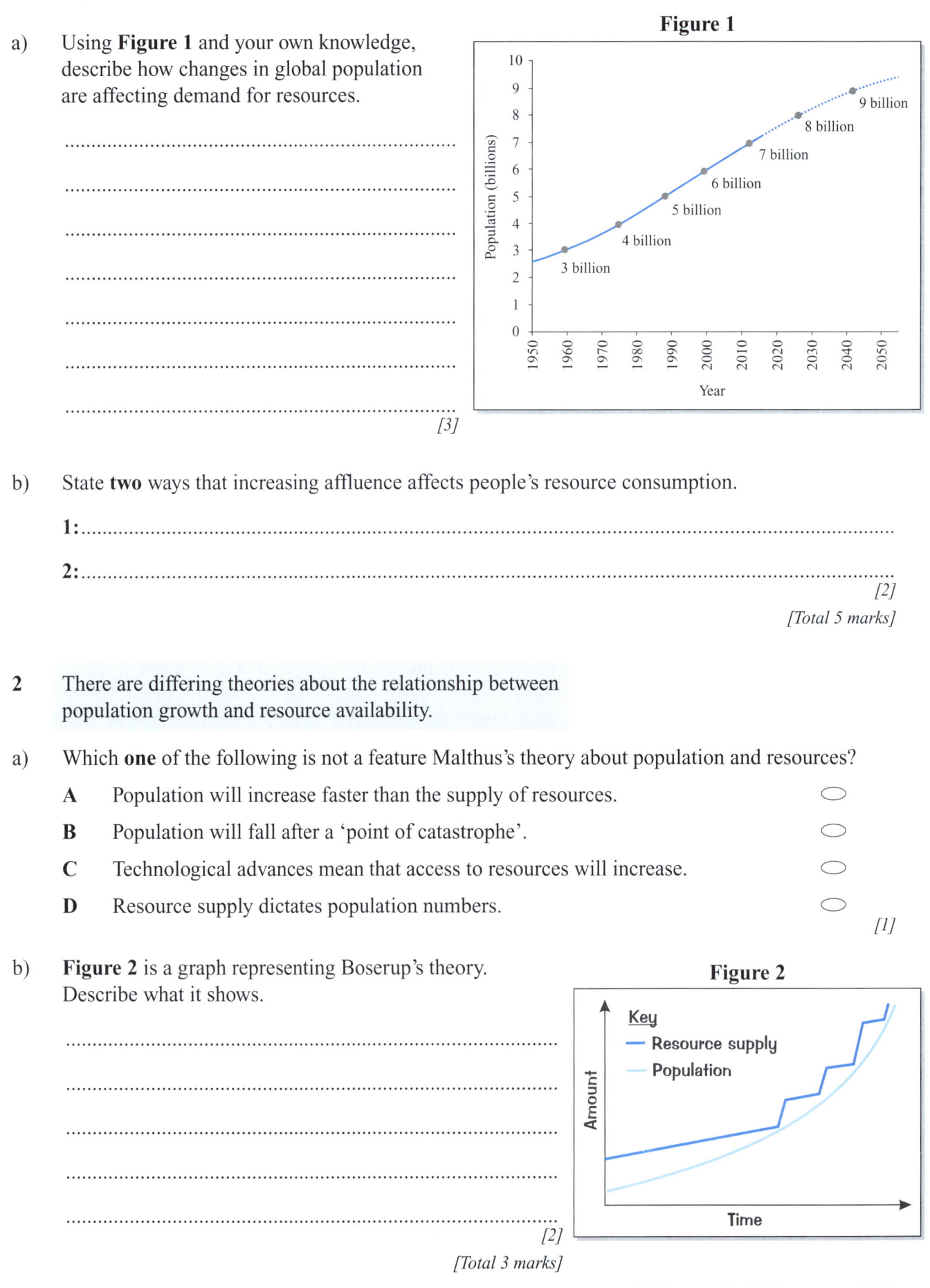

a) Using **Figure 1** and your own knowledge, describe how changes in global population are affecting demand for resources.

....

....

....

....

....

....

....
[3]

Figure 1

b) State **two** ways that increasing affluence affects people's resource consumption.

1: ....

2: ....
[2]

[Total 5 marks]

2 There are differing theories about the relationship between population growth and resource availability.

a) Which **one** of the following is not a feature Malthus's theory about population and resources?

  A Population will increase faster than the supply of resources. ◯

  B Population will fall after a 'point of catastrophe'. ◯

  C Technological advances mean that access to resources will increase. ◯

  D Resource supply dictates population numbers. ◯
[1]

b) **Figure 2** is a graph representing Boserup's theory. Describe what it shows.

....

....

....

....

....
[2]

Figure 2

[Total 3 marks]

Topic 7 — People and the Biosphere

Topic 8 — Forests Under Threat

Tropical Rainforests

1 Study **Figure 1**, a diagram showing layers of vegetation in a tropical rainforest.

a) Using **Figure 1**, state the physical conditions in the layers labelled A and B.

Figure 1

A: ....

....

B: ....

....
[2]

b) Explain **two** ways that trees in the layer labelled A are adapted to their environment.

1: ....

....

2: ....

....
[4]

c) Explain **two** other ways that plants in tropical rainforests are adapted to their environment.

1: ....

....

2: ....

....
[4]

d) Using **Figure 1**, suggest how animals that spend most of their lives in the layers labelled B and C may be adapted to the conditions found there.

B: ....

....

C: ....

....
[4]

e) Suggest how the soil and plants in tropical rainforests are dependent on one another.

....

....

....
[2]

[Total 16 marks]

Tropical Rainforests

2 Study **Figure 2**, a diagram showing how nutrients are cycled in a tropical rainforest.

a) Which of the following is the process occurring at the arrow labelled X?

    A   Leaching ◯

    B   Precipitation ◯

    C   Surface runoff ◯

    D   Rock weathering ◯

[1]

b) Name the nutrient store labelled Y.

....
[1]

c) State the form in which most nutrients in tropical rainforests are stored.

....
[1]

d) Describe how nutrients are transferred along the arrow labelled Z.

....

....

....

....
[2]

[Total 5 marks]

3 Tropical rainforests have high biodiversity.

a) Define 'biodiversity'.

....

....
[1]

b) Explain why high biodiversity leads to complex food webs in tropical rainforests.

....

....

....

....

....
[4]

[Total 5 marks]

Topic 8 — Forests Under Threat

Threats to Tropical Rainforests

1   Study **Figure 1**, a series of maps showing the extent of deforestation in an area of tropical rainforest between 1966 and 2016.

Figure 1

1966 1976 1986

1996 2006 2016

Key: Forested   Deforested

a) Using **Figure 1**, describe the changes to the rainforest between 1966 and 2016.

....
....
....
....
....
....
[2]

b) State **two** possible reasons for the deforestation of the area shown in **Figure 1**.

   1:..

   ....

   2:..

   ....
   [2]

c) Explain **two** environmental impacts of deforestation.

   1:..

   ....

   ....

   2:..

   ....

   ....
   [4]

d) Explain how climate change is an indirect threat to tropical rainforests.

   ....

   ....

   ....

   ....

   ....
   [4]

   [Total 12 marks]

Topic 8 — Forests Under Threat

Tropical Rainforests — Conservation

1 Study **Figure 1**, a graph showing the rate of deforestation in an area of tropical rainforest.

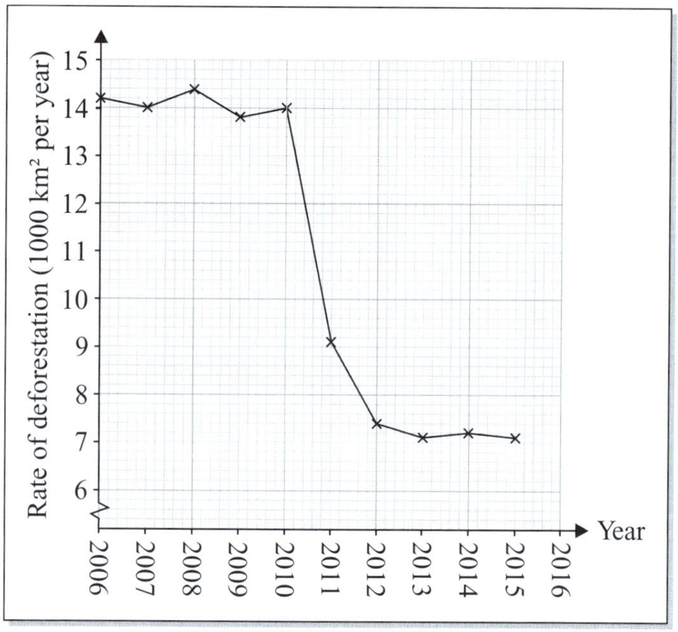

a) What was the rate of deforestation in 2008?

....
[1]

b) Complete the graph to show that the rate of deforestation in 2016 was 6 800 km² per year.
[1]

c) Calculate the percentage change in the rate of deforestation between 2010 and 2014.

Figure 1

(Graph: Rate of deforestation (1000 km² per year) vs Year 2006–2016)

....
[2]

d) Identify **two** possible reasons for the trend between 2009 and 2013.

1:..

....

....

....

2:..

....
[2]

e) Describe **one** global action that could help to reduce the rate of deforestation.

....

....

....
[2]

f) Identify **one** advantage and **one** disadvantage of your chosen global action.

1:..

....

2:..

....
[2]

[Total 10 marks]

Tropical Rainforests — Conservation

2 Sustainable forest management can be used to conserve tropical rainforests.

a) Which of the following best describes a way of managing tropical rainforests sustainably?

   A   Remove all trees in an area.   ◯

   B   Replant deforested areas with a single tree species.   ◯

   C   Only cut down and remove older or weaker trees.   ◯

   D   Use large machinery to take trees of a single species.   ◯

   [1]

b) Explain why it can be a challenge to make sustainable forest management schemes successful.

   ....
   ....
   ....
   ....
   ....
   [4]

c) Explain why promoting alternative livelihoods might be a better way of protecting tropical rainforests than sustainable forest management.

   ....
   ....
   ....
   ....
   ....
   [4]

d) State what is meant by 'ecotourism'.

   ....
   ....
   [1]

e) Explain the benefits of using ecotourism to promote conservation of tropical rainforests.

   ....
   ....
   ....
   ....
   ....
   [4]

   [Total 14 marks]

Taiga Forests

1   Study **Figure 1**, a photograph of a snowshoe hare, and **Figure 2**, photographs of trees found in taiga forests.

Figure 1

Figure 2

a)   Explain **one** way in which the snowshoe hare shown in **Figure 1** is adapted to its habitat.

....

....
[2]

b)   Explain **two** other ways in which animals can be adapted to survive in the taiga forest ecosystem.

1:...

....

2:...

....
[4]

c)   Explain **two** ways in which the trees shown in **Figure 2** are adapted to their habitat.

1:...

....

2:...

....
[4]

d)   Describe **one** example of interdependence between plants and animals in taiga forests.

....

....
[2]

[Total 12 marks]

Topic 8 — Forests Under Threat

Taiga Forests

2 Study **Figure 3**, a diagram showing the interdependence between biotic and abiotic factors in taiga forests.

a) Identify which of the following statements is true.

- **A** A and C are abiotic factors. ○
- **B** B and C are abiotic factors. ○
- **C** C and D are biotic factors. ○
- **D** A and D are biotic factors. ○

[1]

Figure 3

- A: Cold, dry climate
- B: Few species of animals
- C: Soil low in nutrients
- D: Plants grow slowly

b) State where most nutrients are stored in taiga forests.

....
[1]

c) Using **Figure 3** and your own knowledge, describe how the climate can affect the soil fertility in a cold environment.

....

....

....
[2]

[Total 4 marks]

3 Taiga forest and tropical rainforest ecosystems are very different.

a) Identify which of the following statements is true.

- **A** Biodiversity and productivity are higher in taiga forests than in tropical rainforests. ○
- **B** Biodiversity and productivity are lower in taiga forests than in tropical rainforests. ○
- **C** Biodiversity is higher, but productivity is lower in taiga forests than in tropical rainforests. ○
- **D** Biodiversity is lower, but productivity is higher in taiga forests than in tropical rainforests. ○

[1]

b) Explain the difference in the levels of biodiversity in tropical rainforests and taiga forests.

....

....

....

....

....
[4]

[Total 5 marks]

Threats to Taiga Forests

1 Global warming is an indirect threat to the biodiversity of taiga forests.

a) It is thought that global warming is increasing the frequency of forest fires in taiga forests. Explain the impacts of this on biodiversity.

....

....

....

....

....
[4]

b) Explain **one** other way that global warming is threatening the biodiversity of taiga forests.

....

....

....
[3]

[Total 7 marks]

2 One major threat to taiga forests is the exploitation of the fossil fuels found underneath them.

a) Explain the direct threat to the taiga forest caused by the exploitation of fossil fuels.

....

....

....
[2]

b) State **two** other ways that humans exploit the resources available in taiga forests, which cause a direct threat to the forests.

1: ....

2: ....
[2]

c) Explain how burning fossil fuels can threaten the taiga forest ecosystem.

....

....

....

....

....
[4]

[Total 8 marks]

Topic 8 — Forests Under Threat

Taiga Forests — Conservation

1 Study **Figure 1**, a photograph of an area of taiga forest in a national park.

Figure 1

a) What is a 'national park'?

....

....

....
[1]

b) Explain the benefits of creating a national park.

....

....

....

....

....
[4]

c) State **two** challenges that may be encountered in managing taiga forests.

1:..

....

2:..

....
[2]

d) Explain how sustainable forestry could help protect the taiga forest.

....

....

....
[2]

e) State **two** reasons why people may object to setting aside protected areas in taiga forests.

1:..

....

2:..

....
[2]

[Total 11 marks]

Topic 9 — Consuming Energy Resources

Impacts of Energy Production

1 Energy can come from renewable, non-renewable or recyclable sources.

a) Identify which of these energy sources is a recyclable source.

- A   Fossil fuels ○
- B   Solar energy ○
- C   Nuclear energy ○
- D   Wind energy ○

[1]

b) Which of these statements about renewable energy sources is true?

- A   Renewable energy sources can be replenished as quickly as they are used. ○
- B   Renewable energy sources take millions of years to form. ○
- C   Coal and oil are renewable energy sources. ○
- D   Renewable energy sources are often extracted from the ground. ○

[1]

c) State why non-renewable energy sources are sometimes described as stock resources.

....

....
[1]

[Total 3 marks]

2 Study **Figure 1**, a photograph showing an energy source.

a) Identify the energy source shown in **Figure 1**.

....
[1]

b) State whether the energy source shown in **Figure 1** is renewable, non-renewable or recyclable.

....
[1]

Figure 1

c) Name **two** other energy sources of this type.

1: ....

2: ....
[2]

d) Explain **one** negative environmental impact of exploiting the energy source shown in **Figure 1**.

....

....

....
[2]

[Total 6 marks]

Impacts of Energy Production

3   Study **Figure 2**, a map showing proposed energy production sites in a coastal area.

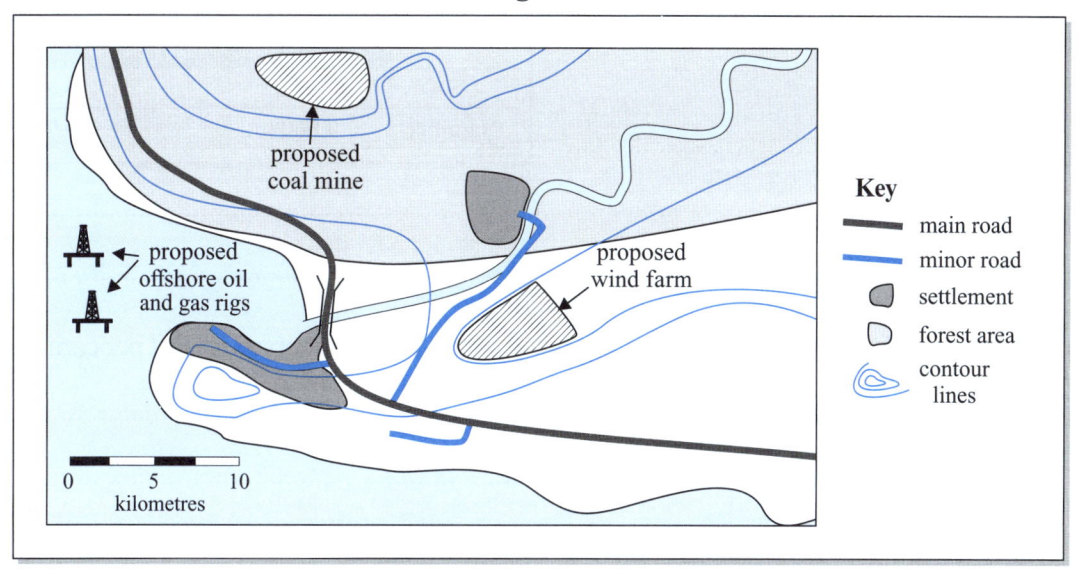

Figure 2

a)   State **one** environmental impact that mining for coal may have on the area shown.

   ....
   ....
   [1]

b)   Explain why there are environmental concerns about offshore drilling for oil and gas.

   ....
   ....
   ....
   ....
   ....
   [4]

c)   Suggest why there may be objections to developing a wind farm in the area shown.

   ....
   ....
   ....
   ....
   ....
   [4]

   [Total 9 marks]

Access to Energy

1 Study **Figure 1**, a table showing GNI per capita and energy consumption per person in 2012 in the USA and Namibia.

Figure 1

	GNI per capita (US $)	Energy consumption per person (tonnes of oil equivalent)
USA	52 620	6.81
Namibia	9 060	0.72

a) Suggest **one** reason for the difference in energy consumption between the USA and Namibia.

....
....
....
[2]

b) Explain what might happen to Namibia's energy consumption per person if GNI per capita increased.

....
....
....
....
[3]

[Total 5 marks]

2 Study **Figure 2**, a map of Barmouth Bay, Wales.

Figure 2

a) Which location, A-E, would be the best site for an onshore wind farm? Give **one** reason for your choice.

Location:...
[1]

Reason: ....
....
....
....
[1]

b) Suggest why location E is not suitable for a solar power plant.

....
....
....
....
[2]

[Total 4 marks]

Topic 9 — Consuming Energy Resources

Oil Supply and Demand

1 Study **Figure 1**, a data table showing the amount of oil produced and amount of oil products used in Brazil and Sudan and South Sudan.

a) Calculate the difference between the amount of oil produced and the amount of oil products used per day in Sudan and South Sudan in 2008.

Figure 1

| | Brazil | | Sudan & South Sudan | |
Year	Oil produced (1000 barrels per day)	Oil products used (1000 barrels per day)	Oil produced (1000 barrels per day)	Oil products used (1000 barrels per day)
2008	1812	2205	478	94
2009	1950	2481	483	125
2010	2055	2699	486	115
2011	2105	2777	453	111
2012	2061	2923	112	107
2013	2024	3033	247	107
2014	2255	3144	259	108

....
[1]

b) State **one** possible reason for the decrease in oil production in Sudan and South Sudan in 2012.

....
[1]

c) Brazil has oil reserves of around 15 billion barrels. State what is meant by the term 'oil reserves'.

....

....
[1]

d) Calculate the percentage change in oil products used in Brazil between 2008 and 2014.

....
[2]

e) Brazil is an emerging country. Explain why the amount of oil products used has been increasing.

....

....

....

....
[4]

f) In 2008, there was a global financial recession. Explain how this recession may have affected oil prices.

....

....

....

....
[3]

[Total 12 marks]

Increasing Energy Supply

1   Study **Figure 1**, a photograph showing an oil drilling facility in a remote area of Alberta, Canada.

Figure 1

a) Identify **two** economic benefits to Canada in exploiting the oil reserves in the Alberta wilderness.

   1:..

   ....

   2:..

   ....
   [2]

b) Other than economic benefits, state **one** reason why oil and gas sources are being developed in ecologically-sensitive and isolated areas.

   ....

   ....
   [1]

c) Alberta has also begun exploiting unconventional oil and gas sources.
   Name **one** unconventional oil or gas source.

   ....
   [1]

d) Explain the environmental costs of developing the energy source you chose in part c).

   ....

   ....

   ....

   ....

   ....
   [4]

   [Total 8 marks]

Topic 9 — Consuming Energy Resources

Sustainable Energy Use

1 Study **Figure 1**, a bar chart showing the breakdown of an average person's carbon footprint by source in the UK.

a) Define the term 'carbon footprint'.

....

....

....
[1]

Figure 1

Average UK carbon footprint (bar chart showing Carbon dioxide (tonnes) by Source: Recreation ~1.95, Heating ~1.5, Food ~1.4, Household ~1.35, Hygiene ~1.3, Clothing ~1.0, Commuting ~0.8, Air travel ~0.65, Education ~0.45, Phones ~0.05)

b) Using **Figure 1**, give the biggest contributor to the average individual carbon footprint in the UK.

....
[1]

c) Using **Figure 1**, how much CO_2 does commuting contribute to the average individual carbon footprint in the UK?

.... tonnes
[1]

d) Identify **two** strategies that an individual could use to reduce the carbon footprint of their house.

1:..

....

2:..

....
[2]

e) State **one** way that the energy efficiency of transport in the UK could be improved.

....

....
[1]
[Total 6 marks]

2 Many countries rely heavily on fossil fuels for their energy rather than having a diverse energy mix.

a) Explain how diversifying the energy mix can improve energy security.

....

....

....

....
[3]

b) "Alternatives to fossil fuels should be developed." Assess this statement.

[8 + 4 SPaG]
[Total 15 marks]

Topic 9 — Consuming Energy Resources

Energy Futures

1 There are contrasting views about the sources of energy to use in the future.

a) Identify which of these options best describes the 'business as usual' scenario for future energy use.

    A   The same amounts of fossil fuels are used, but additional energy is generated from renewable sources. ○

    B   Everyone agrees to reduce global energy consumption so that fossil fuels last longer. ○

    C   Most energy is still generated from fossil fuels and the use of renewable energy sources is not increased. ○

    D   The amount of energy generated from fossil fuels is reduced and the use of renewable energy sources is increased. ○

[1]

b) Identify **two** groups who are likely to support the 'move to sustainability' scenario.

1:..

2:..
[2]

c) Explain **one** reason why these groups support a move to sustainability.

....

....
[2]

d) Suggest **one** reason why transnational corporations may support the 'business as usual' scenario.

....

....

....
[2]

e) Explain why the majority of consumers currently support the 'business as usual' scenario.

....

....

....
[2]

f) Explain why there is likely to be a shift in consumer support from 'business as usual' to the 'move to sustainability' scenario in the future as fossil fuel supplies are exhausted.

....

....

....
[2]

[Total 11 marks]

Energy Futures

2 Study **Figure 1**, pie charts showing the proportion of UK energy from different sources in 1970 and 2014.

a) State which source of energy the UK most relied on in 1970.

....
[1]

b) State which energy source increased its share the most between 1970 and 2014.

....
[1]

Figure 1

1970: Coal 47%, Oil 44%, Gas 6%, Nuclear 3%
2014: Coal 17%, Oil 34%, Gas 34%, Nuclear 7%, Wind/Hydro 2%, Biofuels 6%

Key: Coal, Oil, Gas, Nuclear, Wind/Hydro, Biofuels

c) Using **Figure 1**, describe the changes in energy sources in the UK between 1970 and 2014.

....
....
....
....
[3]

d) The changes in energy sources shown in **Figure 1** are similar in many developed countries. State **two** reasons why rising affluence can lead to more sustainable energy use.

1: ....

2: ....
[2]

e) Other than rising affluence, explain why sustainable energy use has been increasing in developed countries.

....
....
....
....
....
[4]

f) Explain why some governments of less developed countries are concerned about having to increase their use of renewable energy sources.

....
....
....
[2]

[Total 13 marks]

Topic 9 — Consuming Energy Resources

Making a Geographical Decision

The issue: tar sands production in the Canadian taiga forest

There are more than 300 million hectares of taiga forest in Canada, covering roughly 35% of the country. One of the biggest threats to the forest is the exploitation of the tar sand deposits in Alberta. Almost three quarters of Canada's indigenous communities live within the taiga forest and their traditional way of life is being threatened by mining activities. However, the tar sands have an important economic value to Canada and mining developments are expanding as more and more companies are investing in the area.

Figure 1: Tar Sand Deposits and Mining Area

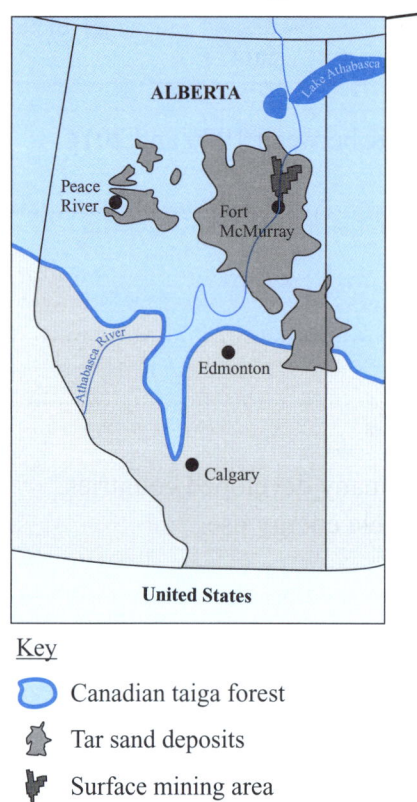

Key
- Canadian taiga forest
- Tar sand deposits
- Surface mining area

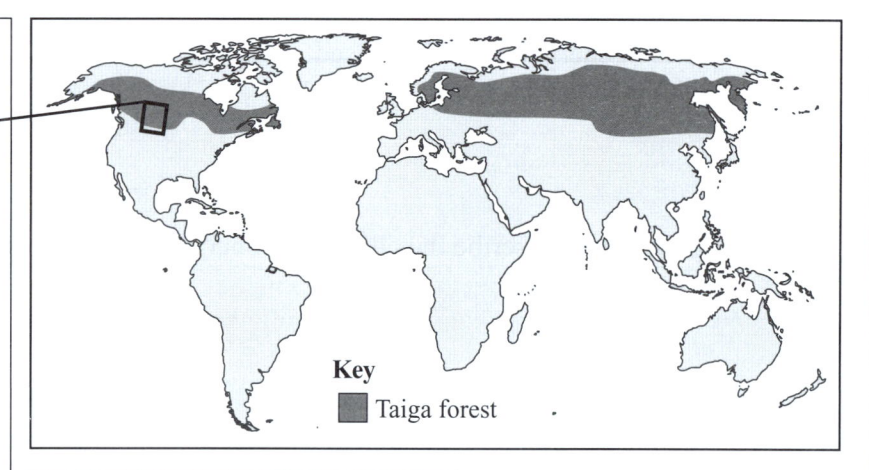

Key
- Taiga forest

Figure 2: Oil Extraction

The tar sands are the world's third largest proven oil reserve and lie under the taiga forest. The sands contain bitumen, which can be refined to produce oil. Sand is collected in surface mines and is then taken to processing plants where the bitumen is extracted using a mixture of chemicals and water.

Figure 3: Human Use of Taiga Forest

Trees are felled for house and furniture building and to make paper. Indigenous communities rely on the taiga forest for food, water and traditional medicines.

Figure 4: Renewable Energy in Canada

Almost a fifth of Canada's primary energy is generated from renewable sources.

Hydroelectric Power (HEP)

Canada is a major world producer of HEP. There are over 600 hydroelectric dams in the country, many of which are on rivers with their source in or flowing through the taiga forest.

HEP has several environmental impacts:

- Changes in water flow can lead to a build-up of silt in reservoirs, which can kill plant life.
- Dams prevent migratory fish from reaching their breeding grounds further upstream.
- The creation of reservoirs is thought to have destroyed almost 13 million acres of forest.

Figure 5: Newspaper article

DAILY NEWS
SEPTEMBER 2014

TAR SANDS PLAY IMPORTANT ROLE IN CANADIAN ECONOMY

New research has shown that tar sands development is boosting the Canadian economy. It's estimated that nearly 480,000 jobs were created in 2012 and that the tar sands industry represented 5% of Canada's GDP.

Investment in the industry is expected to continue increasing in the future as tar sands developments expand — this could create hundreds of thousands more jobs for Canadians. Expansion of mining operations is expected to double industry revenues by 2025.

Making a Geographical Decision

Figure 6: Growth in Tar Sands Production

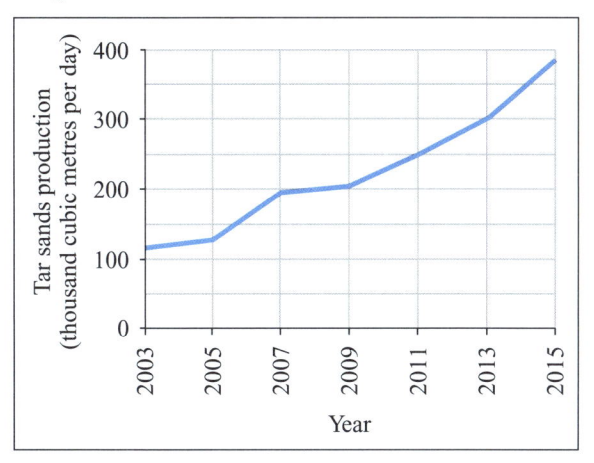

Figure 7: Expansion of mining operations at Fort McMurray between 1984 and 2011

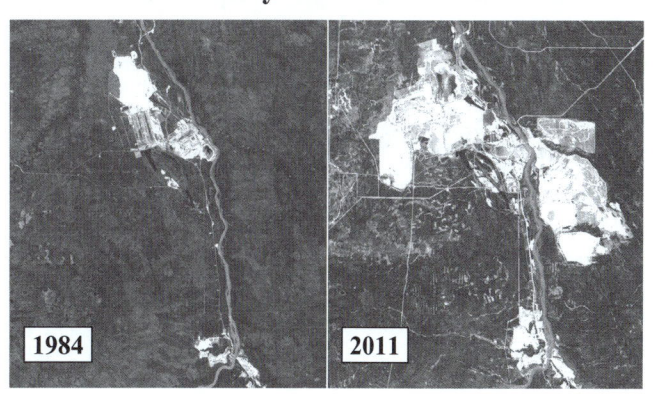

Figure 8: Attitudes towards tar sands production

Tar sands production company	Environmental groups
"The extraction processes we use are carefully monitored to ensure we cause as little environmental damage as possible. We have a responsibility to protect the land for the future."	"Tar sands mines pose a serious threat to the taiga forest. Deforestation is causing loss of habitat and the mines are polluting rivers and other water courses."

Government official	Indigenous communities
"The tar sands are an important sector of the economy and help to provide jobs for thousands of people. Without them, we'd lose lots of investment in goods and infrastructure."	"The toxic emissions from the mines are causing serious health problems in our communities. We rely on the forest for food and water, but it's being replaced by mines."

1   Study the **three** options below for how Canada should develop energy sources in the taiga forest.

   Option 1: Continue exploiting the tar sand deposits to create more job opportunities and further economic growth in Canada.

   Option 2: Place restrictions on the development of tar sands, introduce measures to reduce environmental damage and invest more money in sustainable energy sources.

   Option 3: Stop the development of tar sands and promote the production of hydroelectric power in the taiga forest.

   Select the option that you think would be the best long-term decision for Canada.
   Justify your choice using evidence from the information provided and your own knowledge.

   [12 + 4 SPaG]
   [Total 16 marks]

Acknowledgements

Graph showing the changing area of sea ice on p.7 Data Source: Satellite observations. Credit: NASA National Snow and Ice Data Center Distributed Active Archive Center https://climate.nasa.gov/vital-signs/arctic-sea-ice/

Graph of sea level rise on p.7 adapted from Climate Change 2001: The Scientific Basis. Contribution of Working Group I to the Third Assessment Report of the Intergovernmental Panel on Climate Change. Figure 5. Cambridge University Press.

Photograph on p.10 (Slidell, Louisiana after Hurricane Katrina) © FEMA/Liz Roll

Photograph on p.16 (Montserrat) © Wailunip licensed under the Creative Commons Attribution-Share Alike 2.5 Generic license. https://creativecommons.org/licenses/by-sa/2.5/deed.en

Photograph on p.16 (Nepal) © Krish Dulal licensed under the Creative Commons Attribution-Share Alike 4.0 International license. https://creativecommons.org/licenses/by-sa/4.0/deed.en

Statistics on p.18 (except GNI and HDI) from The World Factbook. Washington, DC: Central Intelligence Agency, 2017.

GNI per capita values on p.18 from The World Bank: Indicators.

HDI values on p.18 from 2015 Human Development Report, United Nations Development Programme from hdr.undp.org. Licensed under the Creative Commons Attribution 3.0 IGO license. http://creativecommons.org/licenses/by/3.0/igo/

Graph of UK airport data on p.23; map of UK population density on p.58 and p.59; deprivation statistics on p.66; pie charts on p.97 all contain public sector information licensed under the Open Government Licence v3.0. https://www.nationalarchives.gov.uk/doc/open-government-licence/version/3/

Graph of world urban population on p.28 based on the data from the United Nations, Department of Economic and Social Affairs.

Data used to construct map on p.28: Human Development Index and its components, United Nations Development Programme from hdr.undp.org. Licensed under the Creative Commons Attribution 3.0 IGO license. http://creativecommons.org/licenses/by/3.0/igo/

Population data in table on p.29 adapted from United Nations, Department of Economic and Social Affairs, Population Division (2014). World Urbanization Prospects: The 2014 Revision, Highlights (ST/ESA/SER.A/352).

Business start up data in table on p.31 source: ONS, Business Demography, NOMIS, Mid-year population estimates.

Photograph on p.x38 (limestone pavement) © Mike Green / p.39 (glacial trough) © Richard Webb / p.39 (meandering river) © Simon Ledingham / p.46 (cliff erosion) © Stephen McKay / p.48 (coastal defences) © Rob Farrow / p.51 (interlocking spurs) © Bob Bowyer / p.53 (Inversanda bay) © Alan Reid / p.54 (gully) © Richard Webb / p.62 (Newcastle Upon Tyne, 2015) © Andrew Curtis. These works are licensed under the Creative Commons Attribution-Share Alike 2.0 Generic Licence. http://creativecommons.org/licenses/by-sa/2.0/

Map extracts on pages 40, 44 and 51 reproduced with permission by Ordnance Survey® © Crown copyright 2017 OS 100034841

Map of over 65s on p.59 source: ONS, WG, NRS, NISRA. Data: Population estimates 1992-2010.

Manchester population data, Manchester job density data, Argyll & Bute job density data on p.60 source: Office for National Statistics licensed under the Open Government Licence v.3.0. http://www.nationalarchives.gov.uk/doc/open-government-licence/version/3/

Argyll & Bute population data on p.60 © Crown copyright, 2017.
Contains public sector information licensed under the Open Government Licence v3.0.
http://www.nationalarchives.gov.uk/doc/open-government-licence/version/3/

Map of UK on p.60 and map of central Newcastle in 2016 on p.64 contains OS data © Crown copyright and database right (2017)

UK migration data on p.61 and graph of London migration on p.65 adapted from the Office for National Statistics licensed under the Open Government Licence v.3.0. http://www.nationalarchives.gov.uk/doc/open-government-licence/version/3/

Graph on p.62 adapted from Welsh Government - Statistics © Crown Copyright 2015.

UK FDI data on p.63 source: Department for International Trade licensed under the Open Government Licence v.3.0. http://www.nationalarchives.gov.uk/doc/open-government-licence/version/3/

GNI values on p.92 from Global Health Observatory country views, © World Health Organisation (2017), http://apps.who.int/gho/data/node.country, accessed April 2017.

Energy consumption per capita data on p.92 based on IEA data from [IEA Statistics © OECD/IEA 2014] © OECD/IEA 2016, www.iea.org/statistics. Licence: www.iea.org/t&c; as modified by Coordination Group Publications Ltd.

Map on p.92 by David Maliphant. Contains OS data © Crown copyright and database right (2017)

Data in table on p.93 source: U.S. Energy Information Administration (Jan 2017).

Graph on p.95 showing average carbon footprint in the UK based on the data from a study by the government-funded Carbon Trust.

Tar sands industry employment and GDP data on p.98 from IHS CERA Special Report Oil Sands Economic Benefits Today and in the future © 2014 IHS.

Data used to construct graph on p.99 from National Energy Board, Canada Oil Sands Facts and Information.

Photograph on p.99: NASA Goddard Space Flight Center. Image credit goes to Rob Simmon and Jesse Allen, NASA's Earth Observatory.